THE COOL GUY'S GUIDE

THE GAME OF ROMANCE

MATTHEW MCCAHILL

&

SPENCER BURNETT

The Cool Guy's Guide
The Game of Romance
All Rights Reserved.
Copyright © 2019 Matthew McCahill & Spencer Burnett
v3.0

The opinions expressed in this manuscript are solely the opinions of the author and do not represent the opinions or thoughts of the publisher. The author has represented and warranted full ownership and/or legal right to publish all the materials in this book.

This book may not be reproduced, transmitted, or stored in whole or in part by any means, including graphic, electronic, or mechanical without the express written consent of the publisher except in the case of brief quotations embodied in critical articles and reviews.

Outskirts Press, Inc.
http://www.outskirtspress.com

ISBN: 978-1-4787-9804-0

Cover Photo © 2019 www.gettyimages.com. All rights reserved - used with permission.

Outskirts Press and the "OP" logo are trademarks belonging to Outskirts Press, Inc.

PRINTED IN THE UNITED STATES OF AMERICA

DEDICATION

Spencer: This is a dedication to every woman who has fallen for a player and tried to convince herself that he's going to change. If being an amazing partner and lover isn't enough to inspire your man to gather all of his creative scheming and sexual energy and point it only in your direction, then this book may be the guidance he needs to be the man you know he can be.

Matt: To my lovely wife—may she read some of these tips and smile, knowing I went the extra mile to make her my wife and be a good husband to her. It's not how we get to falling in love—it's the feeling of being in love that makes us complete and has made us so strong together.

To the men asking the question of how you know she is the right one. It's always the same answer for all of us who have found true love…

We just knew.

TABLE OF CONTENTS

Introduction: You're probably going to Screw this up i

The Five Relationship Phases 1

Set the Spark 13

Stand Out From The Crowd 35

Go From Casual To Committed 77

Deepen The Connection 125

Fuel the Fire 165

Closing: See You Out There 201

Troubleshooting 207

INTRODUCTION: YOU'RE PROBABLY GOING TO SCREW THIS UP

You may be a man that has no problem "picking up" women but that doesn't mean you know how to be a good partner and lover. You may be a traditional "nice guy" but too nice becomes bland, bland becomes boring and boring eventually becomes disinterested. Every man brings something unique to the table but she wants you to have a little bit of everything.

When you finally find a woman that has everything you want there is only one thing that is ALMOST guaranteed: it is going to end in heartbreak. You might blow it by saying something wrong on the first date. You might move in together and realize that your habits aren't compatible. Even if you get married the chances of that working out is 50 percent and out of those who stay married, how many of them are still deeply in love with their partner and still excited to wake up to them every morning?

If you're looking to not screw this up you need to be creative, bold, kind, and considerate. You're also going to have to create boundaries, take time for yourself and sometimes tell her no. You're going to have to take the lead, make decisions and sometimes playfully tug her hair and smack her ass. You're also going to say "yes, dear" and be wrong even when you're right. You need to charm her girlfriends, make her co-workers jealous of your public romantic gestures and make her mom fall in love with you.

Once you have initially won her heart, the game isn't over. To turn this love affair into an incredible relationship, you have to do all the right things at the right times and in this book we're going to show you precisely how to do that.

Lets Cut Through the Crap

Quick aside to say: There is no magic guide or answer to anything, and we're not going to insult your intelligence by pretending you're not savvy enough to know that. We can't guarantee you'll fall in love or stay in love after reading this book. We may not even be telling you anything you didn't already know.

Some of the advice may seem common-sense, but that doesn't mean you commonly display it or even remember it. Even the most thoughtful and diligent of us mess up when it comes to love—a lot. So, it helps to have a guide like this in which the best advice is gathered and always right at your fingertips. Plus, this stuff isn't coming just from our brains and experiences—it's based on the experiences of lots of people, including us. We know these ideas work, and why they work—and once you read this book, so will you.

Why Is There a Game?

Research has shown that couples in high-quality relationships evaluate behavior, set goals, and make changes. Relationship effort is linked to relationship quality. All this means is you get out of a relationship what you put into a relationship. That effort you put in directly correlates to your happiness as a couple. This isn't a book that focuses on the nitty-gritty of scientific studies, so we won't go into more details here, but if you want to do your own studying, there are plenty of books that break hard science into manageable bites.

Making an effort in a relationship isn't just about being partners in the game of life, but it also requires playing a cat and mouse game of seduction. The way that you feel about the connection with someone is always fluctuating. Sometimes you're snuggling after sex and you just want to be there forever, and then there are other times like *Get this chick out of my face. I need some space.* That's natural. So, you've got to learn how to fall in and out of love. When people get complacent in their relationships, they start feeling like they're falling out of love and they start feeling really guilty, so they ignore it, as opposed to stepping into it and making something of it.

The number one reason marriages end is because of infidelity. The problem isn't that one partner is just so insanely attracted to someone else and they just can't help themselves. The problem is they are bored and they feel like the flame in the relationship is out. What we are about to share with you will help to make sure you keep the fire of your relationship white hot and lasting forever.

If you are a successful everyday gentleman, then you probably have dated more than one woman at a time. There's logic to this. You do this because they serve different needs. One of them is a sweetheart, and one of them is the bad ass, and one of them cooks you food. But when you're in a monogamous relationship, you and your partner have to play all those roles, so it has to be dynamic. The key is variety, not newness. It all can exist within your relationship—you just have to build your relationship that way.

Matt's grandfather used to always say, "I don't know ten of 'em who make one good one." He was kidding, of course, but there is always a little truth to every joke. He was saying no one is perfect, and you're not going to get all the best parts of ten women without getting ten parts of the bad.

Even though you're playing a little bit of a game, you're really trying to keep this girl who's perfect for you. So, you need to keep reminding her that you're perfect for her. Now some of our tips might be a little edgy and unconventional. Some of our tips will require you to take charge and play the traditional role as the man, and some of our tips will require you to submit to your woman and let her take the lead. Remember, to keep her interested you have to be a little bit of everything at just the right time.

In this book we are going to be straightforward with you, we're not going to dance around undeniable truths by trying to be too politically correct. Keep in mind, this is a book from men to men so this book has been written in a language men understand and connect with. Although this book was written ultimately to men, this is also meant to help women get a great man. There are a lot of great guys out there that just act stupid and we're putting our effort toward helping these good men show up in a way that makes you fall deeper in love every day.

How Some of Our Tips Have Played Out

Each story and tip in this book aren't philosophical suggestions that we think will work for your relationship. Every tip and story in this book are from our personal experiences. So they have been tested in our relationship and have proven to be keep the spark in your relationship.

We also love hearing the stories of what happens when people follow our advice. It's usually good, but sometimes something happens that's greater than any of us were expecting. And yeah, we've changed the identifying information in the following to protect the innocent.

The Unexpected Happens

For example, Trev, Spencer's buddy, discovered that he could get more than he expected—in a very good way—when he followed our advice to "Order her dinner and drinks," in a way in which you both listen to your girl's wishes and can take control of a situation.

This tip is contrary to everything we've been told about dating women. Really think about this. Picture it: The server walks up to the table and instead of telling your date to order first—about as much chivalry as we're told we're still allowed to exhibit—you open your mouth and say, "My lovely date is interested in the salmon, I'll have the lamb, and we'll start with the beet salad." The server stands there in the awkward silence. You can tell he wants to say something to your date, but there's nothing to say. Everything's been ordered, and if he asks your date for confirmation, he looks like an asshole. Absolutely no one—not your date, not the server, not you—is used to you and only you speaking.

We gotta hand it to Trev—he did it. He said at first he could feel his date start to freak, but he could also hear her wheels turning: She realized there wasn't really anything she could be pissed about. They'd talked about the menu before he ordered, so he knew she wanted the salmon. All he did was be the one to order it. Then, get this: he actually felt a change in his date. She looked at him a little more intently. By the time he asked her if she wanted him to order dessert, she really didn't want anything but him. She leaned across the table and said, low and sexy, "So, are you this confident in…other places?" And by this time, he *was* confident. He replied with what he'd do to her, and what he would have her do to him, in the bedroom later that night.

Let's just say they made that happen not very much later that evening—his date was like "Get the check. We're going." And that was the kind of take-control Trev wanted from her.

In another example, Matt's got an ex, Jessamine, from college with whom he's still friends. This is a good thing, especially because he gets some great insight on how these tips work with women. When Matt asked her for some feedback for this book, this was the first tip she thought of. Which he thought was interesting—this quiet, simple tip. But there's a reason it's in the "Stand Out from the Crowd" section. It can have serious impact on a relationship.

Jessamine said that her boyfriend had asked her over for a home-cooked meal. They fooled around, they ate, the evening passed, and then he asked if she'd like to go for a walk. She was just lounging in the shirt he'd been wearing—and she said, fine, she was ready. Yes, she assured him, just like that—and asked him to make her a dark and stormy for the road while he was at it. This was an offer he could not refuse. Taking a walk with a sexy lady who was wearing only his shirt, enjoying a little rum as they went? It was after midnight, and he lived in a quiet neighborhood. It was a low-risk but still dangerous-feeling, sexy-feeling move that showed how even a quiet walk could be awesome. What really made the walk special was there were no distractions. They got to focus on one another, have a real conversation and learn more about each other.

Fine-Tuning

Our egos are in check to the extent that we know we can always learn and fine-tune our tips. So, sometimes we learn that guys need to be prepared for the unexpected with these tips. Spencer's cousin followed our advice to "Buy a cheap gift," designed to show that meaningful is more important than expensive.

Every time they passed the bar they went to on their first date, she would point it out. She had nothing to say about it; she just got a little excited every time she saw it. So one day when he was walking by the bar, he stopped. He went inside, ordered a beer, and gathered together a little collection of items: matchbooks, paper coasters, all with the bar's name on them. Back home, he had an old cigar box he kept change in. He dumped that out, put the stuff from the bar in it, and that weekend presented it to his girlfriend.

She opened the box and got the strangest look on her face. Once he confirmed that she wasn't angry but confused, he set about figuring out what was so puzzling. "You know," he said, "our place? The bar we went to on our first date?"

She started laughing. "Oh! That's its name? I didn't remember!" So he missed one step and didn't set up the gift with a story of their first date and where they went. That's OK—anytime we can make the one we love smile is a win.

She still liked the gift, but the impact had a little less oomph and a little more oof. That's the thing about gifts that rely on meaning—the giver and the receiver may assign different meanings to different things.

Or take, for example, the time this guy we both know tried to "Send her creative social media messages." From his experience, we learned to offer a word of caution about this: do not—man, do *not*—engage her friends online. We both know a guy who treated his early online interactions with his woman like any other interaction. Damn, was that a mistake. All of a sudden, he's in an argument with her mother, and they've never even met. Then his woman's sister jumps in to try to side with both of them and just shut the situation down, and then he's arguing with her. OK, come to think of it, the guy is kind of a hothead this woman is probably better off without (yeah, she dumped his ass right after this). In short, just don't. The point of this is to connect with her in all places, IRL and virtual—not to wave your peacock feathers around, showing off your opinions and mansplaining her right out of your life.

Matthew suggested a tip to one of his friends that he write "I want your body" with your finger on the bathroom mirror before she takes a hot shower. The steam will reveal the message long after he left for the day. Except, get this: it was too generic a note for his friend's lady, and it totally backfired.

She had stayed over at his place the night before, and he needed to get out the door first the next morning. So they did the weekday morning shower dance (no, not that kind, unfortunately), him showering first and then her going in. He wrote his note after he'd dressed and then he took off, calling out to her to just lock up with his spare keys when she went and he'd get them back from her later. He wanted her to spot his message after he'd already gone, so she'd think of him again.

A couple hours later, he's hard at work, and his phone starts ringing. He sees it's his lady and decides it's worth taking a break to answer. He's expecting all sorts of happy sounds from her and promises about how she'll show him her adoration later. Instead, she starts yelling at him! Turns out she assumed his message had been written not by him but to him, from some other woman.

Thankfully, he calmed her down. The next time she stayed

over, he made sure to repeat that morning, but better. He wrote a much more explicit message, one that could only be from him to her, and then he signed it with her nickname for him. That got him the phone call at work that he wanted.

In All Seriousness

We're good-natured guys, so we (try to) put a lot of humor in this book and keep it light. But the results are serious, no matter how much fun the results are, it's still good to highlight some of the heartfelt stuff.

Like Spencer's client who met his girlfriend at a meditation retreat halfway around the world. It was one of those all-inclusive, no-phones, no-regular-clothes places that totally cocooned you from the outside world. You also weren't allowed to talk to anyone else there. So, it wasn't like his future girlfriend was strutting around for him in her best Friday night outfit, and it wasn't like either of them were wooing the other with their sparkling wit. Yet somehow they connected. They think it had to do with their minds being on some different plane—and connecting, naturally, without conscious thought. To this day, they continue to meditate together, following our "Meditate together" advice, every morning before work and then once a month for one solid day. We don't know if this is the key to their success as a couple, but we don't doubt their happiness, and they're still going strong after many years.

We also offer a tip to "Make a home porno." We love putting this story in the same "serious" category as the meditating tip, but it belongs there—and not just because the same couple who meditates together also told us they'd taken our home porno tip. That's right, and we don't find it all that surprising. Both meditating and making such a movie are incredibly intimate acts (that can also be rather transcendental). It's hard to give as many details about this tip as the meditating one, but let's just say...know your acrobatic limits. You knew we would get a laugh even in the serious section of this book, did you?

Hilarity

Speaking of laughing, sometimes the stories are pretty hilarious. For example, Matt's friend, Kyle, took his advice and gave his woman a call between meetings one day. This is found in the tip: "Make a five-minute FaceTime Call." This tip is used to show her you care and also that you're not going to always adjust your schedule for her.

When she received the FaceTime, she was so happy that she was practically purring: "Oh! You're calling me just because? On your way to a meeting? That's so sweet!" He altered his schedule not one second, and she hung up feeling like he'd moved the world for her. Of course, then his brain was at least a little distracted from work, and get this: as soon as he hung up with his girl, his phone rang, and he answered it with "Hey, babe." And, you guessed it, it was his boss asking him to bring something for the meeting.

Or what about when Spencer's client, Jake, who followed our advice to "Provide service after the sale." In order to treat her well from start to beyond finish in the bedroom, you have to first know how to help her finish, and that is part of this tip. Well, this one woman Jake knew was, let's just say, supersensitive—even a breath on the right spot could set her off. And how would she express this? Through laughter. A little unnerving at first—*hey, I'm working hard here, lady!* But by pushing his ego aside, Jake pretty quickly got it. This was pleasure, just escaping in laughter.

One of our tips is to "Give an emoji a secret meaning just for you and her." No, stud, this is not the time to mess with the poop emoji, even though that would be really funny. Instead, be like Mike—literally, our friend Mike. Mike's a bouncer at one of the clubs Matt works with. In other words, this dude is tall and built. He's got a super deep voice. When he's not at work, he rebuilds muscle cars and plays in high-stakes poker games. We're not kidding when we say this guy is an uber male. He's also got a sense of humor. So, one night he and his girlfriend are texting each other, and he just pulls out one of those ridiculous emojis that no one understands what it means, that one with hands sort of waving in front of its face, and sends it to her with the caption "Jazz hands will get you the happiness you want tonight."

She practically choked on her wine, she was so caught off guard. It was very simple, but it charmed the nightie off her—literally. She replied, "Get over here. Now." The jazz hands emoji became their one-click secret saying for "I want to please you tonight."

We also have a funny story about "Give an end-of-night butt massage." Um, OK, this is a good one. One of our friends did this, except he did not study up before he dove in. And his lady was too sweet to say anything even though it must have hurt like a mother...because she woke up the next morning with two new dimples on that cute little behind of hers. Specifically, two little bruises from that love lug's having pressed too hard. She was thinking of him at work all day...because it hurt every time she sat down!

DON'T STOP BEING A PLAYER— JUST PLAY A DIFFERENT GAME

The game of seduction lasts forever, but certain "plays" shouldn't. Most guys simply focus on the short game but every guy has his own approach, each one has his angle. We know these guys—we may have even been these guys.

There's...

The One in the Know: On so many levels, this is a great guy. He's charming and witty and pays attention, but he's not using his skills for good. He's not playing the long game, just trying to get some tail.

The Name Dropper: He's the guy who brags all the time. He has so many women—or claims to, which means he might be a poseur.

Mr. I'm Buying: He might be mean, ugly, and stupid, but he's got cash, so he gets women. He knows that alone won't take him to forever with a girl, but he doesn't know what else to do.

The Cheeseball: In fifty years, he'll be pulling quarters from your ears. This guy is a dork but not in a charming way.

The Mr. Nice Guy: He's the guy agreeing with everything his girl says. His mantra is "whatever you want to do." He gives his girl everything he's got and never says no.

The Broke Player: He's taking his girls to Olive Garden and loses his confidence every time the bill comes. This is the guy who's trying really, really, *really* hard, but he's going nowhere fast. This kind of effort is misdirected, misses the mark, and exhausts potential lovers.

The Snake in the Grass: He's the guy you'd never expect. He seems like one of the good ones, but he's thinking only about himself and how and when to strike.

The Bullshitter: This guy's got all the right words and all the right moves, but hang out near him for long, and you'll smell the stink.

The Socialite: Yeah, it's great that he's got a wide social circle, until he has no time for his girlfriend. He's always out with the guys, who are sometimes other girls looking to swoop in if there are any cracks in his romantic relationship.

The Social Media Player: This guy makes massive use of modern technology. He's always online, talking about where he is, where he's staying, swiping right.

The Non-Player: You might connect with him on Tinder but he's too busy playing video games to get back to you. He claims that he's "really busy" to make it seem like he's a man in demand

There are lots of different types of guys with short-term goals, but a lot of you share one reason for why you started acting this way: you're always trying to keep yourself safe, protected. It's part of healing yourself to be able to put your heart out there and love somebody—it really is.

You've got to remove those walls—just like the women you're dating do.

Women have the same problems as men in many basic forms of relationships. Finding her out, figuring out what makes her tick, helps you transform from being a player into the stable, life-building partner you're both looking for.

Circles and Rings

Let's discuss two important fears, the fear of abandonment and the fear of suffocation.

The Fear of Abandonment

The fear of abandonment is a big one for a lot of women. The fear of abandonment isn't just with women whose fathers left or who had their heart broken by a shitty ex-boyfriend. Women's primal mind is designed to be concerned about abandonment. It's in the DNA code of being a good mother. So you've got to make sure she knows you are never going to abandon her (that doesn't mean you don't break up or leave her; it means you do so in the right way).

You need to manage the relationship by giving her the support and stability she needs. She knows that and loves you all the more for it since it's so important to her stability. But too much support and constant contact can trigger a whole new problem that is just as bad.

The Fear of Suffocation

Matt's parents, who are still together after decades of marriage, went to couples counseling in the '80s, and their sessions had a big impact on the whole family. He still thinks about some of the insights they learned and shared with their kids. One was about the circle inside another circle:

being the circle around somebody else's circle doesn't work, for either person.

No matter how in love you are, she cannot be your entire life, and you don't want to be hers either. You're suffocating or being suffocated. Either way, if one of you can't breathe, the relationship will die. Instead, you and your partner want to be like the Olympic rings, looping together, touching but independent. You overlap in places, but you do not inhabit all the same spaces.

Having your own life, having your independence, is huge, especially when you're at about the six-month point in the relationship. You're in love, and you're starting to integrate your life with hers. Your weekends become her weekends, your friends become her friends, your hobbies become her hobbies and vice versa. The bonding is great, but there needs to be some things that you do separately, so you can come to the table with different outside experiences. That enriches both of your lives!

You also need to build and stabilize trust in a relationship. If you've been a player, or been seen as one, you have to earn trust more than other guys do. (That doesn't mean you have to always make grand gestures to prove you're trustworthy. For example, not having a lock on your phone is a great way to show your lady that you have nothing to hide.) But when we talk about building trust, we don't just mean on your part alone. We mean both of you in the relationship. If you can't take a trip with your buddies without her throwing a fit because she doesn't trust you, then you have to put in some serious work with her. We're not talking staying home and showing her you love her—instead, still go on that trip *and* prove to her that you're thinking of her. She may not like it, so be gentle. You shouldn't have to check in with your girl, but if she is feeling worried, then it's the right thing—just not every night and not every trip. Make those check-ins on your terms, but make her happy, so you can build that trust and continue to build the relationship. This is a great opportunity to show your friends that you are serious about your girl. Be open about your relationship. You have to be there for her but you also have to be there for yourself.

Even at the beginning of the relationship, you can't just sit on the sidelines. The relationship starts the moment you notice a girl. At this point, you should be thinking not only with your heart but with your brain. Use your perceptive skills to pick up on the things that are going to bug you later before you get too emotionally involved. Conscious decision-making is always better than emotional. Think about the flashlight keychain and candy bar you picked up while in line at the convenience store. You impulsively buy crap you don't even want just because it's in front of your face. The strongest circles and rings are formed if your relationship starts from a mindful place, not an illogical "oh, why not" place. Basically, pick the girl you want, not the one who is just there in front of you.

It's Never Too Late to Play Smarter

If you're in a relationship and have found some of your power slipping away, it's not too late. Figure out where your place is now, and if you're in a good spot, great. Keep it. If you're in a bad spot--if she's walking in front of you, if she's talking over you, then you need to fix that. (But she better not be interrupting and taking over the conversation, or you are gonna have a serious uphill battle.) I'm not saying you need to start talking over her. The goal is to keep it balanced, walk together side-by-side; she picks the restaurant one day, and you pick it the other.

In each phase of a functioning relationship as laid out in this book there are examples and tips to create mini-experiences that shape a healthy relationship. When everything is said and done, all you have left are the stories of those experiences. Those memories are the stories you get to tell your children, family, and friends for the rest of your life. When you're at the end of your relationship, that is all you have. Your couple's story is made up of these experiences. If you're writing the story for that girl, you want it to have a diversity of scenes, just like in the movies. No woman wants to just watch romantic movies. Women love watching dramas and comedies, and everyone loves a good thriller. A director surprising the audience is not a bad thing. They're doing it to create an experience. Again, all of these tips that we're using, they're just elements to create those stories. Like we said, your woman wants to feel it all, and so do you.

This is the story of your relationship—not just the stuff her friends will highlight in a photo montage at your wedding reception. This is the stuff that will get you to that wedding.

The following strategies are your story expressed through the emotional tactics you use to check in on your partner, check in on yourself, and check in on your relationship. Using these, you'll either grow your relationship or realize the end has come. If she isn't the one, it is better to find out now rather than waste time because things are "comfortable."

The key to having a successful relationship is to continue to play but change what you brag about. You used to brag about the model you had sex with in the bathroom or the foursome you had on Halloween, but now you get to change your standard and brag about how good you are to your girl.

A Story from Matt

I was walking from one bar to another with a group of friends in Nashville, and I noticed one of the girls was walking three steps ahead of her boyfriend but reaching back, saying, "Grab my hand."

I leaned over to him and told him not to grab her hand but catch up to her and then put his arm around her shoulders and his hand on her far shoulder. I said, "I want you to do this instead of what she wants, which is to pull you from place to place, and I want you to slow her pace down to yours as you walk together."

I knew this couple from being around them a few times, and this girl is dominating, assertive, and outspoken, so it put a smile on my face to see her boyfriend take my advice. Once he did, she turned into a content, sweet girlfriend who cuddled up next to him and waited for him to lead her. It was just a simple change of how to walk, but it made all the difference.

Some women want the freedom to take the lead but even those women are craving a man to take the lead himself. Sometimes it might feel counter intuitive because you want to respect her nature and serve her but sometimes serving her looks like switching between the power dynamics.

THE FIVE RELATIONSHIP PHASES

A relationship follows
five distinct phases:

- ✓ Set the Spark
- ✓ Stand Out from the Crowd
- ✓ Go From Casual to Commitment
- ✓ Control the Flame
- ✓ Fuel the Fire

Most people are good at the first one or two, but you have to guide the relationship differently in each phase, starting with lighting the spark and separating yourself from all the other guys through to locking down the relationship and giving her everything she ever wanted.

You should always treat your lady with respect, but you shouldn't always worship the ground she walks on and be available at her every beck and call. You definitely shouldn't act like she's the only one in charge of the relationship (which she will be if you put her up on that pedestal all the time). So, between meeting her and knowing you're in this for the long haul, you need to put her in her place—and stay in yours. Your relationship is about treating you both as grown-ass adults in a partnership, not you as the adoring schoolboy and her as the queen.

Over the years, you may have dated lots of women in different ways. Some were flings, some serious relationships, and a bunch somewhere in between. When you fall in love with a woman and get married, it will be because of the constant ebb and flow of who was taking the lead in the relationship.

Sometimes she's going to put you in your place, and sometimes you're going to take charge. It's always pushing and pulling, leading and following. It's the mix of: "Hey, the door is open. You have the freedom to leave whenever you want," and, "Where the hell are you going? You're my girl." The game of love and infatuation lies in the discernment of when to play each hand.

You know the value of taking charge of the situation and being a leader, but you'll find, in each of the five phases described in this book, that it's also about putting yourself in a place of submission. However, be cautious. Falling in love has a way of making a man weak. It's crazy: one day you are in complete control of your love life, and almost instantly your balls have been removed and you are completely owned by your other half. But if you were to ask a woman's honest opinion, she would say she doesn't want to run the relationship either. She wants a partner who is an equal and still leads the relationship. She's looking for a man who is brave enough to show his own manliness and not constantly be asking, "Is this okay with you?"

Though you need to be strong and flexible in all of a relationship's five phases, each phase has unique characteristics. Here's a teaser about each phase, and the rest of the book breaks them down with specific activities. At the very end of the book, we offer a Troubleshooting section—a short index of common situations (like, your girl is acting needy) that directs you to a few tips you may find useful in each situation.

THE FIVE RELATIONSHIP PHASES

IGNITE THE FIRE

Increase the significance you have in her life but don't make it evident that she has you hooked. Make her work for it a little bit.

At this stage in the relationship, you've gone out with a woman three or four times, and you're head over heels. Commonly called the honeymoon phase, these first two or three weeks of dating are sweet (don't forget a little bit of spice). You're getting to know each other and putting your best foot forward. But being on your game does not mean letting her walk all over you. This is also the stage when you're establishing that you're not a doormat. In this section, we suggest you:

- Express the typical and expected while doing so in a new and interesting way.
- Find moments that can be memories and act on them.
- Read your woman. If she is used to being taken out and shown off, then invite her to places where no one else is around and keep her all to yourself. Be original in dates and keep it casual.

Stand Out from the Crowd

Now that you have her attention, make sure not only that you're the best but that she knows you are one of the few instead of the one of the many.

Okay, now it's clear you two are dating, but you're not necessarily exclusive, or if you are, you're still early enough in the relationship that a breakup won't feel like the end of the world. You still need to hook her, but—continuing the fishing metaphor—don't let your own line unravel in the process. Our ideas, such as the ones below, wow her and maintain your strength.

- Drop subliminal hints of your relationship, so she will smile when she sees them, without realizing you've laid those clues. Keep her thinking about you.
- Break out of your shell. Do things with her you may not normally do or that you may even hate to do. Make her happy by saying yes to things she wants instead of only doing what you want.
- Show her your softer side, or if you are a softie, show her your masculine side. Express the depth of personality you have.

THE FIVE RELATIONSHIP PHASES

GO FROM CASUAL TO COMMITTED

Show her you're the man and turn up the heat. If you want this woman in your life, this is the time. You've been dating three to six months—it's shit or get off the pot, right? The tips in this section, like the following ones, get her to stay. Let her behind the curtain. Let her in deep to see your vulnerable side—but also start breaking out your best stuff.

- Bring her around your family. Holiday season is great for this, and it's also an opportunity to start new traditions with the girl with whom you're going to spend the rest of your life.

- Invite her out to hang with your friends. If you're ready to let her see you and your friends, that means you're really comfortable with her and expect a lot of her. She'll rise to the challenge of that responsibility and commit to you.

- *Really* tell her what you do for a living. Your woman may know *what* you do for a living but she may not know what your day-to-day looks like. The deeper the details the deeper the intimacy.

Deepen the Connection

How do you get someone to think the world of you? If you're not a playboy, you need to learn how to do this—and know that it's okay to want this.

- Get her to tell you more about herself than she has told anyone else. Listen and learn. Be sure to write it down in your phone under her name in the notes section, or however you want to store it. This information is going to come in handy a month or two down the road.

- A story from Matt: I still have written down the dates of my first kiss with the woman who is now my wife, the first time I said I love you, and the first time she did. No, she didn't say it with me. Hmmm…maybe she was playing the game a little there. I didn't think about that.

- Touch her often and in different ways (that aren't creepy).

- Prove your reliability and stability, that you're attentive and amazing.

THE FIVE RELATIONSHIP PHASES

FUEL THE FIRE

Now that you've got her longing for you, remind her how much you desire her.

- Massage and kiss her over the back of the sofa. This move is all about timing, which shows you care.
- Have a fashion show. Appreciate the fruits of her shopping trips.
- Learn the names of her extended family. Intimacy is emotional as much as it is physical. You can impress her just by paying attention.

As you read through these tips, you'll see that most of them could easily happen in any of the stages, not just the one we've assigned each to. Think about the effect that sending flowers to her work has when you're "the new guy" she's dating and the effect it has when you're the guy who's been with her for years. New-guy flowers show there is a new man in her life, and everyone at her office is now fully aware she is dating someone else. Guy-for-years sending flowers to her work reminds everyone what a great person she is dating. His bouquets also lower the self-esteem of the workplace rats who are sniffing around the female colleagues for loneliness, so they can swoop in. Both kinds of flowers show her she's important to you and give you influence on her feelings, but they have unique emphases.

A Note about Taking Notes

Some of the tips in this book require you to remember details about your lady's likes and dislikes, her day-to-day life, and important dates in your relationship. But we know you aren't going to remember all that crap. Don't worry—there's an easy fix. Take notes. Use the notes function in your phone and your calendar. You know you're not going to remember on your own, so writing it down is essential. Just don't do so in front of her.

Also take notes on the info in this book. Develop your muscle memory by rereading this book. Stick a few of the romantic gestures we suggest in your calendar as future reminders. After you put the book down, you are more likely to actually do a few of them if you have already taken the first step and highlighted her name and clicked edit to add a note or clicked "calendar" or "notes" on your phone.

Okay, get on out there. Two important last reminders: One, a lot of these tips suggest you make a move in a situation. Then, you've always got to listen to her response. If she's not interested at that moment or in that activity, accept that. Maybe try again another time or in another way. Communication and consent—always. And two, don't ever forget your intentions, even when your lady starts plucking your heart strings. When you start to really feel something for her, you are going to want to bend your rules to

THE FIVE RELATIONSHIP PHASES

conform. You cannot do this. Love takes time to percolate. Remember, you're in this for the long term. Here's to you beating the odds against the inevitable.

SET THE SPARK

Month 1

- ✓ Stand out from the pack
- ✓ Be a classic gentleman
- ✓ Keep her on her toes
- ✓ Allude to your softer side

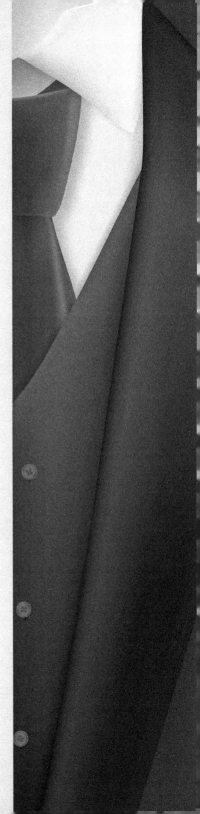

This is the phase where you get to use all your patented moves. The only difference is you're using them to entice her to be your girl for the long run…not just to sleep with her.

At this point, a few guys might be courting her, so you need to stand out from the bunch. Now, you don't have to be better, you just have to be different in a way that makes her want to keep paying attention. In this phase, your actions don't have to be over the top, just outside the lines of typical guy behavior.

You can use some of the same moves that other guys do—you just have to do so creatively. In the beginning of a relationship, she isn't going to continue with the "guy she's always wanted." Rather, she's going to pursue the man who is unlike any other man she's seen before. She's not looking for the best-looking, most educated, or most wealthy. What she's really looking for is something that her girlfriends can't get.

This phase is a tricky one. If you come off too soft and predictable, she will feel like you are just like every other thirsty loser who's trying to get in her pants. If you come on too strong or you're trying to win her over by buying extravagant gifts, you're going to look like one of those douchebags trying to quickly get laid.

The key is to use subtle elements: be a little soft and a little bit of a bad boy and be creative in a way that makes her want to brag to her girlfriends and her social media following.

It's best to show all your sides during this phase. So, if you're known as a bad boy, when you are on a date, show her your more tender side. Give her light kisses periodically, hold hands, and bring a single flower on your date. If you are more of the nice guy, then be a little bit more assertive and bolder in the way you compliment her. Let her know how that dress she's wearing is interfering with your ability to listen to her talk about her day. Playfully tap her ass as she walks past you when you open the door.

The point of the first few dates is to help her realize that she was wrong when she thought she had you all figured out. So many guys struggle with this because they want to lead with the side of their personality that feels most natural and authentic. Remember that you aren't just trying to sleep with this woman, but you are trying to entice this woman through intrigue so you can have a long-lasting, stimulating, and fulfilling relationship.

A woman initially wants a man around with whom she can fully feel like herself, but once she's completely comfortable being herself, she's going to yearn for a man who can pull out sides to her personality she's never expressed before. All good girls want to be freaks sometimes, and all freaks want to be good girls. If you demonstrate that you are a man who openly expresses all elements of his personality, then you are setting the foundation for her to explore her own unique and extreme versions of herself. We'll get more into the details of this later, but the first few dates are about setting the framework and foundation on which the relationship can flourish.

Tips

INITIATE THE FIVE-MINUTE VIDEO CALL.

Calling her will make you stand out from 99 percent of men because no one picks up the phone to call anymore. When you get on the call, make sure you let her know that you only have a couple minutes, but you just wanted to see how she was doing. Most guys make time for women they are crazy about and show this by being willing to rearrange their schedules and make these women the top priority. Calling your woman between meetings lets her know that she's important enough for you to pick up the phone during your busy workday but not so important that you would missing work obligations for her.

SET THE SPARK

A Story from Spencer

Whenever I start courting a woman I follow her on Instagram. Now most guys will make little comments or send messages trying to engage with her.

Remember the goal is to stand out. So instead of typing messages I will randomly video conference them on Instagram. You can do this on FaceTime or Facebook video as well. Most men don't have the creativity, courage or desire to put the effort to put themselves out there like this.

When I call I just tell them that I have a few minutes but I just wanted to see her face. That sets the frame for you to have some meaningless chit-chat. Early in the relationship, it's not so much about what you talk about but more so about how you make her feel while you're talking.

Ask questions that no other guy has asked her.

What was the last non-sexy Halloween costume you wore?

Have you ever stolen a piece of candy from a convenience store?

If there were a karaoke machine here right now, what would be your first song?

This is all about diving into the nooks and crannies that make her the woman she is today. This will make you stand out from all the other lame dudes asking her about what she does for a living, where she went to school, and whether or not she has any brothers and sisters. Ask her about parts of herself that seem insignificant. If you see significance and have interest in the things she doesn't even think about, she's going to start wondering, in a good way, "Who is this guy?"

Buy a cheap gift.

Buy something that is more meaningful than expensive. This demonstrates that your thoughts and creativity drive your actions, and money is just a simple tool to help you shape your story.

> *A Story from Spencer*
>
> *The very first date I went on with my girl was during the holiday season. We went to the city for a light lunch and then walked downtown to look at all of the Christmas lights and displays in the department store windows.*
>
> *She was from Miami so she didn't really know how to dress for the cold. So we took I city stroll into a department store to buy her gloves and a hat out of necessity.*
>
> *She was still cold so went into Walgreens to buy a few heat pack hand warmers and a cheap scarf. It all cost under $50 but it was the fact that I was thinking on my feet to make sure she felt comfortable. You don't have to buy designer threads in order for her to cherish them. The joy is in the story not in the actual items.*

BE PLAYFULLY RUDE.

Find a reason to reach over her to grab something. On your way back to sitting, pause by her ear and say in a sexy, soft voice, "Excuse me," and then smile.

If you've just worked out, make sure you shower before this. But this works great before you've put on any cologne. Let her smell you. You do know about pheromones, don't you?

PLAN THE ONE-HOUR DATE.

Have her meet you between meetings or for lunch. This date shows her that you are a busy man, but you will find time for her even when there is no chance of sex.

SET THE SPARK

MAKE RESERVATIONS FOR LATE IN THE NIGHT, SO YOU CAN BE THE LAST ONES TO LEAVE.

There is something romantic about closing out a restaurant. You're getting dessert as the staff is cleaning up, and it's just you two in the whole place. The beginning isn't bad either: Think about coming into a dimly lit restaurant toward the end of the evening when everyone is finishing up. You get the ambiance and the great food, but you beat the line and the crowded tables, and you can talk with your date without yelling over the loudmouth two tables over. Make sure you pay the bill with dessert, so the server isn't waiting all night to close out—and tip well.

ORDER HER DINNER AND DRINKS.

This does not mean to order for her and be that guy who tells a girl what she wants. Be a good date and have conversation with her, but at the same time, drop hints about how annoying the girls are who like to order the most expensive thing on the menu. Then talk about what she is having. Find out what she is going to order and then recite that back to the waiter to look like a gentleman that is also taking hold (not control) of the situation.

Listen and ask questions about how she orders, so you know what she generally likes, and pick up on any dietary restrictions she has and remember them. You're not doing this to tell her what to eat and drink but to treat her, to take little decisions off her shoulders, and to show her you've been paying attention to what she does and doesn't like. Order dessert so you don't look cheap. It will make the date last a little longer, and even though women say they don't want dessert, what they are really saying is "You order dessert, and I'll have a bite." It also gives her permission to indulge.

SEND HER CREATIVE SOCIAL MEDIA MESSAGES.

Like it or not, life happens as much online as it does offline these days. Until you start living together, you and your lady may learn about each other's lives mostly by checking each other's online updates. So make sure you talk directly to her online. Spend fifteen minutes making a Snapchat or Instagram story for her. She sees what you've been up to—and her friends can too. (You know how important her friends' approval is.)

> *A Story from Spencer*
>
> *I send messages on social media that seem overly elaborate. I'll choose a few songs that I think that she might like and create a little music video.*
>
> *Other times I would create sexually ambiguous messages using emojis that she'd have to think about to figure out what I'm saying.*
>
> *Another classic is sending a slightly inappropriate video that was only one second long and disappeared after watching it.*
>
> *I was dating a woman that I could only see once a month. Doing little things like this kept her entertained and intrigued. I'm sure she was talking with other guys at this point but my creativity is what made me stand out from the crowd.*

Fix her hair.

We like this gesture because it is a physical flirtation and a sign of caring, all in one motion. If there's a strand of hair in front of her eyes, with a gentle touch move it behind her ear if it's long enough, or just smooth the piece back into the rest of her hair.

The sexiest moves are so slight they don't even register as moves to the opposite sex. Over time, something like this won't be a move but a part of your demeanor.

Massage her head.

Cozy up and play with her hair for at least half an hour. This may sound boring, but most women think this feels great. Run your fingers through her hair, so her scalp can feel it.

This does not apply to girls with weaves or hair extensions. Girls with extensions may be sensitive about you playing with their hair. If you don't know, then you need to know: don't touch the weave!

SURPRISE HER WITH SWEETNESS.

Bring your hands to her waist and move close behind her. Once you have completed the smooth slide-in from behind, lift your other hand to her hair (keep your fingertips on her hips the whole time), and bury your face in it. It's not about smelling her hair as much as it is her hearing you smell her hair. (But don't give a big old snort, sport—keep it nice.) As she turns her face a little to look back at you, smile and maybe even give her neck a little nibble. What you do next depends on the level of friskiness you're both feeling.

Provide service after the sale.

Keep treating her well even after she comes. A back rub after sex is awesome, for example. This tactic is for the highly skilled. (a) You have to know how to give her an orgasm. (b) She has to have one, and you have to know when she does. (c) You have to have enough stamina and selflessness to give her a back rub after all that. But if you can pull this off, she'll forever be your biggest fan.

Long before you try this activity, figure out the answers to points A and B mentioned above. No question is stupid when it comes to sex and understanding what works for your woman. Do some homework on your own and encourage your partner to be open with you every time, not just the times you're really trying. Learn her body. Ask her questions, even while you're having sex—unless she seems to already be headed toward an orgasm, of course. In less intense moments, find out where she is in her head and what she is focusing on to get to the climax. Invite her to tell you things. You can make it sexy. She doesn't have to say, "Please move an inch to the right." Let her know a little moan turns you on, and her noises will direct you to what works for her.

Point C is important too—don't forget about it. A back rub is a beautiful thing, but if you apply the wrong pressure or you have clammy hands or a hangnail that will scratch her, it won't be the best it can be. Keep massage oil, simple hand lotion, even coconut oil by your bed to use in these moments. (Those feel good for her and also mask any dryness or oiliness of your palms.) Listen to her to be guided on pressure. Why a massage, you may ask…Wouldn't you want your girl to rub your back and or feet after an amazing BJ? We do.

Plan ahead for this. Do this tactic after she has been out with her girlfriends while you stayed home. Sober is the way to go to get the G-spot merit badge.

Throw her robe and towel in the dryer before she takes a shower.

Pull a resort-hotel move. Throw in the towel and robe and get them nice and warm. Then pull them out as she's getting out of the shower. The warm, fresh-smelling linens will make her feel like she's in a spa, even for just a moment. And you may get invited to watch her dry off. If she does this for you too, then you know she's gaining points on being the one.

As stated earlier, write "I want your body" with your finger on the bathroom mirror before she takes a hot shower.

The steam will show the message when she gets out.

Give an Emoji a Secret Meaning Just for You and Her.

Could be romantic, sexual, funny, anything. Break it out once in a while, not all the time. You don't want it to get stale. Be ready for her to take it to another level—eventually she'll act that emoji out, you stud. And be happy she is texting you, not some other dude.

Do the Dishes...Together.

Think about how much your lady would appreciate the intimacy and help. Pick up the towel and dry something or put the rinsed dishes in the dishwasher when she hands them over to you. Just being there, next to her, assisting, puts you way into the black in the romance ledger. It's called being engaged. We don't realize it, but the more we sit on the couch while our girlfriends or wives run around, the more we distance ourselves from the ones we love so much and who love us. So many of these tips are meant to keep you off the couch and keep her in tune with you and only you.

Walk with her as if it is a dance.

Hold hands, guide her through a doorway, walk on the side with the traffic, and put your hand on her waist as you stand by her side.

Walk on the traffic side.

Trust us—it's sweet. It's also the gentlemanly thing to do. If a car is about to hit her, you have to be able to push her out of the way, and if you are closer to the buildings, that means you are pushing her into the street, which would not be very helpful.

Walk through a revolving door first.

She shouldn't have to push the door for you.

It's also proper etiquette for you to walk in front when you two are descending stairs. This way you can catch her if she starts to fall. For that reason too, walk behind her up the stairs.

When it's windy, walk in front.

This way she won't feel the brunt of the wind. Ask her to wrap her arms around you, and it will help the both of you. This is mainly for our Chicago friends, but it's good for all to know. Being a human shield is primal.

STAND OUT FROM THE CROWD

Months 2–3

- ✓ Keep her off your top-priority list.
- ✓ Become a part of her daily thoughts.
- ✓ Solidify your sex life.
- ✓ Hint at a future together.

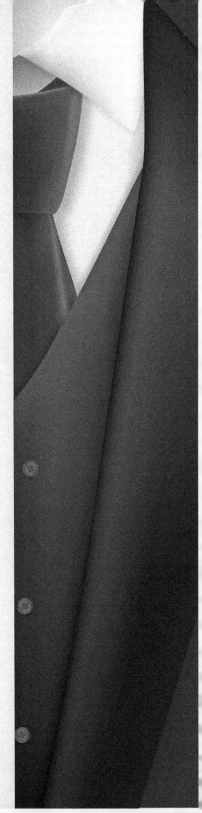

At this point, things are going well. You've had some memorable dates and your sex life has begun to spark. Once you've stood out from the pack, she's going to prefer your attention to that of everyone else who is chasing her. Now it's time to get her invested in your courtship. She will be thinking about you throughout the day. She's going to stop playing games like telling you maybe for a date or waiting all afternoon to answer your text messages.

During the first few dates, she became intrigued. That means that she's paying attention, but she's not quite sold. Now, most chumps in love press the gas and shower her with affection and willingness to be at her beck and call. You know the power of simply disappearing a while to drive her crazy. If you want her to take you seriously, you have to play both sides. The key is to give as much as you can to her while strategically giving her space and time. Her mind will obsess over you while she wonders where you are and what you're doing.

This is the phase where you show her what it would be like to be your girlfriend. When you're with her, be 100 percent in. Stay off your phone and give her your undivided attention. If she is still seeing anyone else, memories of your behavior will occupy her brain even when she's out with him.

But when she's invested in you, she will naturally lose interest in other guys, and she's going to push all of her chips into the middle of the table in hopes of being with you.

The biggest challenge of this phase is in giving her space as the spark between the two of you begins to fire. Typically, when a woman catches feelings for you, it's easy for you to show disinterest because you have other women waiting for your call and dozens of prospects that you've been scouting, but this girl is different. You actually want this woman and nobody else. Don't get caught up in making her the center of your world just yet. Even if this woman is perfect in every way, she hasn't earned the right to be the primary focus in your life.

Stoke her desire to be number one in your life while making it extremely clear that she's not—yet. Her competitive nature will accelerate her desire to be with you. The more used to getting her way that she is, the stronger this effect will be. This takes a delicate balance of giving her your best stuff yet being too dedicated to your own path to be making touches all throughout the day.

Tips

EMBRACE IN THE ELEVATOR.

You don't have to dance in public—a hug in public is just as hot. Pull her to you in an elevator even if there are people there, and if it feels right, kiss her on the lips, maybe the neck. There's no need to get sloppy. No one else is getting hugged in an elevator that day, so the simplest of embraces will make your girl feel held above the pack.

A Story from Matt

Make this count by doing it on a bad day. I once traveled out of state with a girl for an interview for a job she really wanted. It was in New York City, so we decided to make a weekend out of it. The thing neither of us anticipated was her being told that same day of the interview that she did not get the job.

We could have let frustration overwhelm us, even shorten the trip. Instead, we made our way to the hotel. Don't get me wrong—we weren't happy. I let her stew in the cab to the hotel. I continued to keep quiet as we settled in and began dressing for dinner. However, once we stepped into the elevator, I eliminated the silence by pressing her against the wall and kissing her hard. "You're hired," I said. "I'm so excited for our weekend together." You see, she was feeling rejected, and once the right time presented itself, I made her feel wanted…by me.

You constantly have to be paying attention to what she is experiencing in her reality. Excitement is about polarization. If you notice she's feeling rejected, do something that makes her feel wanted. If she's feeling sad, do something that makes her happy. If she's doubting herself bring her into a situation that makes her feel confident. Notice we didn't say "tell her". We told you to DO something. Love is expressed best through demonstration not through simply saying the right thing.

Have sex at a drive-in.

We know what you're thinking. Drive-ins don't exist (at least, not in most places). Hold your horses and keep reading. What was good enough for the pin-ups and their stud muffins is good enough for you, isn't it? This is for the old souls who should have been born fifty years ago. But there are no more drive-ins…or are there? Find a lookout, and with an iPad or laptop, make your own drive-in. Put the computer on the hood if it won't fit on the dashboard and snake the speakers inside. Don't forget to charge your battery beforehand—though if you're doing things right, you won't be watching the movie for long.

KEEP A SEXUAL IDEA BOARD.

Writing down all the things you want to do together will help you learn about each other's sexual desires and fantasies, will help you to not forget your or her good ideas, and will give you the room to think up wilder and wilder ideas. Each of you can even do online sexual scrapbooking—create virtual bulletin boards of images, videos, links to toys, whatever you want. Then look at your boards together.

STAND OUT FROM THE CROWD

A Story from Spencer

I dated a girl for a couple of years, and at the beginning of the relationship, we had sex any chance we could. We did it at friends' houses, on a boat, outside in an alley, in the closet at a toddler's birthday party, and in countless unisex bathrooms across the city. One day we were trying to recall all the places we'd had sex by making a list in a notebook. As we were making the list, we started coming up with places that we'd like to have sex that we could cross off at a later time.

As we continued to check the boxes, we started documenting some of the unique situations and different ways we were having sex, like using sex toys or trying crazy positions, like the Reverse Pile Driver. Soon our sex life became like a kinky scavenger hunt, trying to find more outrageous places and ways to get our freak on.

> *At the end of the relationship, we had over 500 items on our list and over 350 of them checked off. Our sex life never got stale because we were constantly working on this "sex task list" project together. We would update the book every couple of weeks, talking and reminiscing about all of the great sex we had and documenting any kinky new stuff in the book. Because we were constantly either fantasizing about new things to do or fondly remembering and capturing our sexual adventures, this really kept the spark alive throughout the years.*
>
> *That of which gets tracked gets accomplished. If you want to have a stellar sex life, for the rest of your life, documenting your sexual adventures and highlights honors that part of your relationship and keeps certain the flame stays hot.*

REALLY TELL HER WHAT YOU DO FOR A LIVING.

Sometimes the closest people to you don't really know what you do. We're talking details of the daily grind. Maybe you can't explain it easily, so if it's a difficult task, write down bullet points of what you do, so you can have the conversation. Talk about the people in your work life and their personalities.

Ask her to do the same about her job. No, bro, don't ask her to write down bullet points—have an organic conversation. Ask who the people in her work life are and what their personalities are like, so when she talks about work, you can follow the storyline.

Schoolteachers are such great catches, and one of the reasons is they have a story about their kids each day, and it's the same kids each day, so we can easily follow along. It also helps that their main focus is not on an adult named Johnny or something. If your lady does work more with adults than with kids, and Johnny is in her story each day for some reason, keep your cool, man. She still loves you.

Buy her some bubble bath and leave the container on the counter for her to find.

The idea of letting her discover the gift is what counts. Don't be a happy dog wagging his tail with a present for his master but a thoughtful boyfriend who took the time to get something she will appreciate. Leaving it on the table will make her wonder a little bit. She won't be sure if it's for her, so her feminine traits will take over, and she will have to get to the bottom of why there are bubbles on the counter. Use her curiosity to your advantage and let her play into your plan. When she comes to ask you about it, simply say it is for her, as if it were no big deal and just a part of being with you that she gets to benefit from.

BUY HER SOME CHEAP BUT CUTE COLORFUL SOCKS THAT STAND OUT.

She likely will never wear these. That's okay. Every day she opens the sock drawer, she'll be reminded of you, and that's the point of the gift. You need to embed reminders of you into her life just like she has done to yours. We bet you didn't even know she did that, but think of every gift she has given you and how often you see or interact with it. Women are sly, but don't worry. You got this book to help you out.

> *A Story from Spencer*
>
> *Once I was with a girl and she was sick so I went out to buy some cough medicine at Walgreens. While I was there I saw some fleece socks that looked really cozy. I bought 3 pairs of matching designs with different his & her colors.*
>
> *When I showed up not only did I have the medicine but I had a these sock. She though it was so cute. She would wear them every time she wasn't feeling well or if she just wanted to have a slightly better day.*
>
> *Every time she wore those socks she thought of me and the story of getting an unexpected gift. Its good to do things that have her thinking about you all day even if you aren't there.*

HAVE SEX TO MUSIC.

It can be raunchy and fun, slow and soulful, sweet and poppy. It may be all of those—different times, different moods. Just don't be a tool and see how many times per minute you can slam into her. Sex should be more jamming with the music, not slamming to the music.

> *A Story from Matt*
>
> *That reminds me: use music to step up your rhythm game in general. The right kind of beat can help you keep the right kind of time. Here's an interesting bit of trivia about CPR. People are taught to hum "Stayin' Alive," by the Bee Gees, while they give CPR. The beat is perfect for pumping a victim's chest at just the right speed. Well, there is one song said to be the best to move to in the bedroom (or the kitchen or the backseat or...). Hold on to your hat because the song's a shocker. It's "Little Drummer Boy." Yep. Pa rum pum pum pum, baby. Its beat is long, slow, sometimes quick, with some pauses, so it's a good song to play in the background while having sex. Follow its lead.*
>
> *Even the best sex moves gan get boring if there is no variety. Women crave variety more than newness. So be sure you switch it up to keep her mind and her body guessing.*

DISAPPEAR WHEN YOU AREN'T PHYSICALLY TOGETHER.

It's important to allow her to think uninterrupted about you. At this point, her own wondering mind will keep her more engaged than anything you could ever text her. Women *love* to ponder and figure things out. So, give her the space to do that. Make your touches matter. That's why you should make a five-minute call every couple of days instead of sending a constant stream of text messages. This is going to make her anticipate your text. Over time, when her phone vibrates from some other thirsty dude trying way too hard, she's going to secretly hope that it's you, instead of being turned off by the hundredth text you sent that day.

Take her for a walk to nowhere... even just around the block.

If you are a guy who never plans anything, then maybe this isn't the best thing to do, but if you are a guy who plans everything, then it's the best thing to do.

Leave the house hand in hand, maybe with to-go coffees or bottles of water, and just walk. Don't have a plan about where you're going and don't ask which way to go at each intersection. Just...go. You are walking with the purpose of not having a plan, so don't ruin it by asking her which way she would like to go. This is your walk, so own it.

Why walk to nowhere? Because it is about the time you are spending rather than the place you are going.

Red light means stop—and make out.

You and your lady are in the car, you driving and her in the passenger seat. You stop at yet another light. Road rage is building inside you. You feel frustrated. But you don't have to.

Make sure your foot's on the brake—maybe even quick slip the car into park—and lean over and kiss her. And kiss her some more. Keep kissing her till you hear horns. As you shift into gear, say, "Now, that's what red lights are for."

You hate waiting, and making out takes your focus away from waiting for that damn light to turn green. But you know what else that's much more important? Making out gives you two just a few more seconds to connect. Who knows—red-light make-outs could become your thing…for a little while anyway.

Send sweet-nothing texts.

Send her a sweet text like "miss u" or "I want to nibble on your knee right now" and get her stimulated as well as thinking about you. You don't have to use those exact words, but you get the point. When she texts you back, don't respond right away. Take your time. She isn't going anywhere, and just like in fishing, you have to reel her in slowly.

BUILD A FORT AND HAVE A SLEEPOVER.

We're not joking. A quiet night in can really strengthen your bond—even better when the evening doesn't stay so quiet.

> *A Story from Spencer*
>
> *This was seriously my first date with a girl I went on to have a relationship with. We'd met through a dating app and had just been chitchatting online for about a week, not even a phone call yet. She asked what I was doing one night, and I said, "Going to build a bed fort for watching football with my dog. You can join if you like." When she said okay, she'd be right over. I was making a joke, but now that she bought into it, I had to figure out how to build a tent.*

STAND OUT FROM THE CROWD

I attached a binder clip to the middle of a sheet, tied a string to the clip, and then hoisted it up, attaching the other end of the string to the ceiling to form a tent. I met her in my robe—nothing like Hugh Hefner, but the robe had style. I had invited her to bring her coziest of pajamas. We used pillows and blankets and dragged chairs together from all over the apartment. We could have stayed PG only, but...we did end up breaking the main support structure from so much horseplay.

Sometimes the craziest childish behavior can be fun and sexy. Every woman has an inner child that wants to not only be expressed but also wants to be integrated into her sexuality. Play your cards right and you can live out the fantasies she had before she really understood what sex is.

YouTube some Mozart.

Give her a little cuddle time, and you'll benefit within about three symphonies.

Seriously, it's good to try new things and catch her off guard a little, and that's the real point of this tactic. The point is if you already listen to Mozart all the time, put on some Metallica.

This one takes the right timing. You may need to already be relaxing on the couch around the time she comes over. Have her sit with you. Don't lie and say this is your jam or that you listen to it all the time. Be honest and say you are trying something new.

BE IN THE RELATIONSHIP WHEN SHE IS NOT AROUND.

There are some things you have to be careful to tell your girl. There is just too much information that will never help your case. You might think if she knows other women find you attractive then she will be impressed, but the opposite will happen. She will think you are putting yourself out there.

We should never talk about the girls who hit on us. What we should do is embrace the moments when we can show these would-be home-wreckers that we are better guys, monogamous guys. Say with a smile, "Are you hitting on me?" and then politely let her know you are in a committed relationship. Then tell a story about how great your relationship is just to confirm to her that you are not available. Take these moments to prove your love and then never let your lady know. It's not about her knowing. It's about your actions when nobody's looking. We'll tell you this—it just makes you more in love.

It used to be to the story of your conquests to the guys that made you happy inside. It's easy to remember the pride in your voice during those stories. The dirtier the story, the bigger the smile. The pride comes out just as much when the story of your happiness is sincere and to a girl you would have, in your past, been setting up to become a future conquest story. You have had enough of those. It's time to celebrate the love you have found and be 100 percent about your relationship.

Make a bet for Sunday brunch. Loser buys.

Let's face it—you win most of the time, so she is probably going to have to pay. Don't budge. Make her pop for brunch. It's not a bad idea to make the bet something that really neither of you loses—maybe it's about who will wake whom the next morning. This would be a good time to explain how you like to be woken up, if you know what we mean.

Have movie night in.

Ask her what her favorite movie is or her favorite type of movie. Make a note in your phone's calendar and set a reminder for three weeks from when you ask and then invite her to movie night for later in that week. Remember, she wants to have something to look forward to with you, and you want her thinking about you all week instead of one of the other guys scrambling to gain her attention. She will be so impressed you remembered that she won't care that you had to write it down and set a reminder. Oh wait—she will. Better to keep this tip to yourself.

Buy her a new toothbrush.

A person who feels love through gifts isn't typically asking for a piece of jewelry every week—she wants little gifts. To you, it's a two dollar-dollar toothbrush. To her, it's a meaningful, thoughtful gesture that she will subtly think about every day.

For you, it's a way for her to think about you every time she reaches for that toothbrush. She will remember who was so thoughtful and caring enough to buy it for her, and it was only two bucks! Now that's a good investment.

Show her the flowers.

We men don't really get what our women experience, but still try to imagine a scene like this one and what it feels like: Day in and day out you sit at your desk, busting your butt through the paperwork. Every once in a while, the rarest of delivery people, and the most desired, appears in the office, and everyone knows that someone is getting flowers.

The flower-delivery person walks down the aisles, each woman he passes deflating a little. The person he finally stops by is overjoyed. For once, she's the lucky one—and everyone else knows it. The other people in the office feel like they were so close to a little bit of love that when they aren't the recipients, the love feels so far away.

Instead of bringing flowers home, send flowers to your girlfriend's work, so her peers can see how loved she is. This is one of the real reasons girls like flowers. They want the attention, and they want it known that they're so well loved by such a great guy that he sends flowers. Your girlfriend is tired of watching flowers arrive—for someone else, so make her the queen of the room for a day.

STAND OUT FROM THE CROWD

They don't have to be roses. And if you do want to go with roses, don't get red ones unless you have already had the "I love you" conversation. For the first bouquet you ever send her, go really simple and sweet—when you send her favorite flower, even a tiny bouquet works, because you've shown that you've been listening to her preferences.

It's still early in the relationship, so don't go over the top. A $30 bouquet sends the message that you're thinking about her. If you buy the $200 bouquet, it may seem like you're trying to buy her love/attention. Actually, no question it will seem that way.

GIVE AN END-OF-NIGHT BUTT MASSAGE.

This is for you as much as it is for her. They are amazing! You get to grab and play with her butt for twenty or thirty minutes, and she will like it just as much as you do. We carry a lot of tension in our gluteus maximus, but they rarely get the therapeutic attention shoulders and feet do. Win-win, friend.

Despite the fact that the butt appears sturdy, it can be sensitive to massage. If you've ever had a professional full-body massage, you can relate. It takes a bit of time to get used to the pressure of someone pushing on your butt and to unclench. Do some reading up on giving this kind of massage and start slowly once you have your delicious model in front of you.

Ask her how her day was.

It's disingenuous and monotonous to keep asking the same questions each day, so take it a little more seriously today. But not too seriously. Don't make it sound all dramatic. You're just expressing honest interest in her.

Get her to take time out from what she is doing and sit her down next to you on the sofa. The point is to be less predictable this time and more genuine. "Hey, babe," you might say, "let's sit down and talk about our days today." Ask the names of the people in her day, so you can ask about them again tomorrow or a week from now.

If you can't get her to sit down for two seconds, drop it and move on to the rest of your day. Try again another day. Don't give up on this. Your attention is the most valuable thing you possess. Only give it to people and things you love.

FIND A WAY TO HAVE A ROMANTIC KISS IN THE RAIN.

This is the stuff movies are made of. Rain or snow don't have to spoil a date night. It is important to have some ideas at the ready to make a more interesting and longer-lasting memory. Although you've thought about this ahead of time you want it to have a certain level of spontaneity. Pull her into an alley and gently press her against the wall for a hot kiss on a cold, rainy night. Or do what's not obvious in a gentle snow and get ice cream and sit on the hot hood of your car.

Don't do this on the way to a party or other event. Her mind will be on that—and then after you've delayed her in the rain, her mind will be on how her hair is ruined. This is a move for the end of the evening or for when you were caught in an unexpected shower while running an errand.

Offer her your jacket or sweater or at least your scarf afterward.

Keep a couple blankets in your car. That's just smart thinking no matter what, but in this case, she'll appreciate the dry warmth after the heat of the rainy kiss. The blankets should not be sitting on your seat but in the trunk, so it doesn't seem staged. (Of course, we don't want to seem prepared for everything, so if no blankets, then no blankets. Still, try this.)

Care if she got some dirt on her clothes. Just because she's sad about that doesn't mean she doesn't love the gesture, or you. You weren't rolling around in a mud puddle, so any mess won't be big, and you two don't need to dwell on that—just hear her and acknowledge her. Besides, now you two have a reason to take your clothes off as soon as you get inside.

The point of this tip is to make everything worthwhile. Even if it's raining. It's also to add great memories, and most of all it's to show you don't mind getting wet to get a kiss with her. Emotional output drives the sexual tension to a momentous level. You can't mind getting dirty to get dirty.

Change the screensaver on her computer to a pic of you as a couple.

Choose a picture that will remind her of an amazing memory you two had. You can even stage a photo session. Can't decide among the shots? Well, then use the one of her having fun or smiling at the camera and you looking at her like the nut in love that you are. If you have already given her a physical photo, then write something funny on her screensaver.

Make out at lookout point.

We know, it's been a while since you've done this, or maybe you never have. Well, now is your chance. If you live in the city, you will have to drive a few miles out of town. If you live in Chicago, you might need to find a rooftop. Search online for spots to see the city lights or the stars. Turn on the radio or maybe have a song that means something to you both cued up and just sit back and relax for a minute. Once you have both settled in, lean over and head toward her mouth and right at the last minute, stop. Wait for her to bring her lips to you. Timing this with the song is a plus— what if you kissed right at the high point of a song? What if this song became your "couple's song"?

No pushing for blow jobs, guys. This is for the two of you to have a memory together, not for her to do all the work and you get all the reward.

Well, if she insists, go ahead.

SMACK HER ASS DURING SEX JUST A LITTLE BIT HARDER.

A Story from Spencer

Now keep in mind this tip is for the part in the relationship where you have already been sleeping together for a couple months. So at this point you should know where the line is. Don't be an idiot and take this tip too far and actually try to hurt your girl... that being said women want to push the envelope. They want to feel fear even, as long as they know they're in a safe place.

It's best to have a conversation with your girl before you engage in any more aggressive play than you're used to. You'll find that more women are into it than you think. Just be sure to test the waters so you don't cross the line. If you do happen to sting her a little bit, just rub her little red butt and let her know you will be gentler next time. It's okay to smile when you say that. That was a test smack. You need to know if she likes it harder than you have been giving it to her.

STAND OUT FROM THE CROWD

If you cross the line, I've got a single apology that I tell guys to memorize:

"Oh, baby, I'm so sorry. I didn't mean to cross a line; I just meant to find out where it is. Now that I know where it is, I'll be sure that I don't cross it again."

Be open to communication about this. In a loving, consensual relationship, spice should be okay, but everyone's definition of that is different, and everyone has a different history with it. You can always ask her how hard she likes it if you're skeptical about where the line is.

Turn your bathroom into a spa.

Buy two luffas—those are the lacy puffballs you can find in the cosmetics aisle of your local supermarket. "Wax on, wax off" all over her body. Then ask her to do the same for you.

Honestly, even though we love this tip, showers are one of those places that always sound better for sexy time than they are. Do some prep work to make this happen, so you can play without breaking your neck or getting distracted.

- Dude, clean your tub! Get that ring around it down to a dull gray or remove the kids' toys or any other crap you may leave around the tub; spray down even the shower curtain with some good-smelling cleaner, not that chemical stuff; and for god's sake, remove the hair from the drain. You know what's even worse than seeing a bunch of hair on the shower floor? You don't want to deal with her anger when she asks whose hair is in your drain when it's not the color of yours or hers. You can explain that you didn't clean it since you started dating but that's not gonna wash. Don't start slippin', man. When you were single you didn't care, but all that has changed now.

- Buy some sort of shower mats—for both inside the tub and outside. The one inside doesn't have to look like the ugly one your grandparents have. They make okay-looking ones these days. We like the clear ones that look like river stones or bubbles. It's really subtle, but it'll keep you two from slipping at the most inopportune time. For the outside, ditch the towel you've been using as a mat and get a real one. I'm talking cushy with good fibers that kind of massage your feet as you dry off. If you buy one in white, black, cream or gray, it'll look fine with whatever towels and shower curtain you have.

Consider checking out new shower-head options. We all hate having to move out of the warm water for our significant other, so plan ahead, man. Get that double head for when it comes to keeping two people in one shower warm at the same time. It turns your shitty bath into a spa, and you don't have to fight over the water when you take showers together. There are adaptors you can buy for your one lonely shower head that turns it into two, one of which you can aim short and one long, so neither you nor your lady are left out in the cold.

GIVE RANDOMLY.

Place a giant cookie decorated with a frosty smile in her car. This will give her a big smile too.

Obviously, only do this if the two of you are getting serious—don't be creepy and do it on the second date. The point is to make the effort of showing you got up super early, planted a sweet something for her, and let her find it.

Learn to Make Her a Little Nervous... The Right Way.

When we make women mad, it's usually because we screwed up accidentally, so this time you want to control the environment with purposeful motions that may piss her off a little bit, but she can't get mad at you, or at least not for long. It's all about play. Getting her a little upset is just like making her smile. When you are playing with a woman's emotions, you are using a tool, and it needs to be used appropriately and wisely. Here are a couple ways to manage things:

- You make a dinner reservation, but you don't show. As she is leaving the restaurant, thinking you stood her up, she sees you waiting for her at the door, a limo behind you. She will be overwhelmed as what had seemed like the ultimate in low evenings becomes a thrilling night of splurging.

- You send her a text that says, "We need to talk, seriously. Don't text but call me." When she does, her emotions shot up in a panic, you ask why she didn't like your Facebook post. She will be so relieved that it was nothing that her anger will become forgiveness.

Sometimes you have to draw firm boundaries in your relationship, and it might not seem nice or fun. It can't always be. You're managing your relationship with guidelines for both of you. Her included. You are going to have to enforce them sometimes. These are a couple more ways to manage things:

- If you are on a business call, and she wants your attention, put the client on hold. Then, in a serious tone, let her know that your business is what pays for the nights out, et cetera. It's true, and she needs to respect the fact that even when you are away from work, sometimes duty calls and you have to take care of business.

- Blow her off for a friend who needs you. Make sure she knows that you are there for your friends too, and sometimes it's not about her. Keep her in the dark until you have finished with your friend in need. Once you explain the situation, she has to get over it. It was a good-guy move, so she can't really be mad, even though she is.

- You are inevitably going to upset her, so you might as well learn to do it the right way.

By initiating controlled moments of pissing her off, you will get a glimpse of how she reacts, and then you'll know how to react to that reaction. It's like a sports team giving away their next move. Once you have seen how she gets when she is angry, you can react to it without the emotion you would normally, and thus you can deflate the emotional situation. Once deflated, it hopefully just drops away.

Here are a couple general tips about how to react to her reaction. Don't react to her verbal stabs if you know she is going to go that route or if she is the kind of girl who brings three or four past issues into one argument. Simply tell her you can only debate (not argue) one issue at a time. If only one person is arguing, it becomes comical, but don't do what I do and smirk when she is angry. That only gets her more upset. I once almost lost a finger in a silverware drawer when she tried to slam it on my hand while I was reaching for a spoon.

Make love, have sex, *and* bang the hell out of her.

You used to bang one girl and make love to another and just have sex with some and guess what, so did she. Well, now you have to do all three with one girl, your girl or at least the girl you are hoping to become your girl.

All three styles are important, and none are more important than the other. They can be done together or in different sessions. Be intimate with her in all three ways. Often, making love is for the tender times, having sex is for the day-to-day, and banging is when you're both amped up. As a point of reference, you could make love to her after a date, bang her after going to a club, and have sex before morning coffee. But you may be just as likely to bang as you are to make love after a fight. In other words, don't rely on a pattern, but do read the room.

Making Love

Take time in your seduction and be confident in your actions. Be gentle. Be warm. This is the time to say you love her.

Having Sex

We'll go ahead and say it—this one is a little bit of a maintenance move. That doesn't mean you do it without emotion or with one eye on the TV. We just mean, having sex is what you do when you're not particularly emotional—good, bad, or otherwise—but it is crucial to keeping emotion in your relationship. You brush your teeth to prevent cavities; you have sex even when it's just a regular old day, even if you may not be in the mood, to prevent losing connection with your partner. What you don't want to do is decline her sexual advances. This will lower her self-esteem, and she may not try again.

Banging

You are in control. No, not in charge beyond her consent, but in control. Move her where you want her and determine how slow or how fast your belt comes off. Growl dirty talk. These are not the plans of a control freak but the moves of a man. Moves a woman will respond to and forever want. Always be listening for her guidance, but as long as she wants you making the decisions, do so. Tell her you are going to take her and pull her clothes off with intensity and strength. Be in charge and be a man about it.

GO FROM CASUAL TO COMMITTED

Months 3–6

- ✓ Make her part of your plans for the future.
- ✓ Integrate with her friends and family.
- ✓ Develop unique roles as a couple.
- ✓ Invest in the long-term.

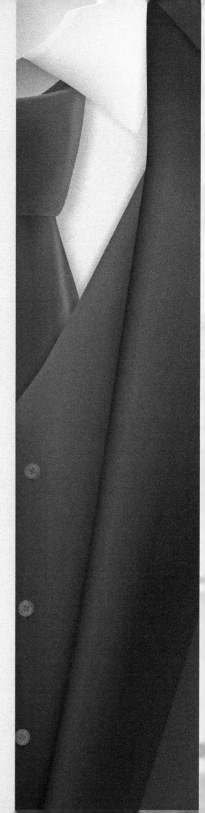

In this phase of the relationship, you may start to wander, not because you are bored but because you are scared that this is getting real. You have to avoid sending late-night texts and scheming how you can see another girl without your girl finding out. You typically do this as a safety net to protect your feelings and to give you the security that if this relationship falls apart, you can deal with the pain by substituting your relationship with a new girl.

Or you have been waiting for this phase and you wanted to lock it up as soon as you met her, but you memorized the five phases and knew you had to wait. Way to go, man! This is the hardest part for players who meet a girl unlike the others and just want to show her how they really are a caring, loving man. You can start now but don't go overboard.

So, now you have had the talk and made the decision together to become a couple. It's time to sink in your hooks (and so will she). The key is to keep your cool. Don't start to pull away but don't dive in too deep. You have been together for a few months now, and it can seem like you have known her for years. This might make you open up more than you should. Keep in mind this is only phase three of five, so take your time to really get to know who she is.

You've dated "stage three clingers" before; remember not to be one yourself.

In this phase, you want to start to integrate with her family, get to know the names of her co-workers, and build relationships with her friends…platonic relationships. You also want to start making plans for vacations and holidays. This is the phase where you really start becoming an "us."

You deepen the relationship by making an investment in her interests. When you connect with the things she loves and genuinely find joy in the process, she feels understood and deeply connected at her core. Be sure to not lose yourself in this. No man is immune from having his testicles removed, because, remember, she's trying to lock you down.

You do all this by putting all the creative energy that you usually put into getting away with wandering into keeping your relationship constantly stimulated with experiences that are not only creative but deeply meaningful. The tips in this section are going to help you with that creativity.

Tips

> **FOR HER BIRTHDAY, GO OUT TO DINNER, BUT HAVE HER FRIENDS MEET AT THE RESTAURANT FOR CHAMPAGNE AFTER DINNER.**

Take her out to dinner, just the two of you. Make it a date and enjoy your time together. Invite the crew to meet you both afterwards. She can invite her friends if that is easier. Her friends will feel included, and she will know you made an effort to make her friends feel included as well. She wants alone time with you, but she also wants her birthday to be celebrated, so this is a good way to do both.

Now, if she wants to keep the party going after the champagne toast, then go for it. But beware, or at least be ready: you are going to become the babysitter for her and her friends, so have fun with that.

CREATE A TIME CAPSULE.

...But only for six months, tops. Things move so fast these days. What should you put in it? Movie tickets, the greeting card she gave you, all the kind of stuff that girls get sentimental about. For this girl, you have kept that stuff. Put it all in a box, and be cleaning your dresser drawers or something one time when she is over. Start reminiscing. "Happen" upon that box and open it as you talk, showing her what's inside.

Then, throw it all away. This is a bonus just to make yourself laugh. Backpedal and say you were kidding; of course you won't throw it away—but don't wait too long. She isn't going to think it's as funny as you do.

Put a note in her jacket pocket that simply says, "I love you."

Or you can just draw a cool World War II tank or whatever it is that you draw really well. Matt can draw a pretty cool tank.

Every time you remind her that you are thinking of her, her heart warms just a little more.

> *A Story from Spencer*
>
> *I once dated a girl who would leave me notes all over the place. She would leave a note under my pillow telling me how much she loved sleeping in bed with me. She would leave notes under my laptop telling me how much she admired my hard work, and she would leave notes in my closet and in my nightstand drawers giving me details on how she felt about our sex life. Some of these notes were so well hidden that it took me a month to finally run into them. It made me feel appreciated every time I found one, although I think that part of her motive was to create "love note landmines" for another woman to find if I were to choose to stray.*

Nevertheless, I realized that leaving these landmines was a great way to invest efforts today that will pay off sometime in the future. I once had a friend hide twenty dollars in his coat pockets as the seasons changed, so the next year he would find pleasant surprises when he wasn't expecting them. Follow that same logic with these notes because maybe she will find one you placed a couple weeks ago at just the right time…like when you royally screwed up.

Romance doesn't have to be about grand gestures. If all you drop is giant love bombs it can look like you are trying a little to hard and that makes you look needy. A few subtle acts of love can be more valuable than a grand gesture.

COME UP WITH A NON-VERBAL WAY TO EXPRESS "I LOVE YOU."

You know, let a smile out after a great kiss—for once, don't hide your emotions.

Move closer to her on the couch, since there is no reason to be so far away. Show her through body language that you are interested in her.

You can't see feelings by themselves. You can see them in body language, which physicalizes your feelings. So always be aware of what your body is saying, in big and little ways. For example:

When you sit side by side, are you leaning toward her?

Are your legs grazing hers?

Do you find reasons for your arm to touch hers?

Imagine the paparazzi taking a photo of the two of you. Would that photo say you are leaning into her or her into you, or would it look like you don't know each other but are just sitting next to a stranger?

Think about how alive you feel the first time a love interest "just happens" to casually touch your arm. What if you kept that aliveness throughout your relationship?

A Story from Matt

A buddy of mine and his girlfriend took a quiz to discover their love languages, how they speak love to someone. Both of them have physical touch in their top two. So instead of always saying, "I love you," which is still important to do, they learned to randomly hug or spend time extra time caressing one another. They both now know that these simple gestures speak volumes without words.

A Story from Spencer

My parents were always role models for me on how two people should love each other in a relationship. They always have done cute things to show their affection. After thirty-plus years of marriage, they still kiss when they say good-bye, hold hands as they walk, and leave notes for each other around the house. They had a little covert way of telling each other how they felt while holding hands: they'd squeeze the other person's hand two times in a row. They came up with this non-verbal way of affection so they could constantly remind each other without using words. Sometimes saying "I love you" doesn't need words.

JOIN A FANTASY FOOTBALL LEAGUE AS A TEAM.

We know, you always do this with your guys, but there's never too much fantasy football. Besides, nowadays it's all on computer, so no shame in your game if your lady doesn't know anything about football (but it's even better if she does).

This is a form of commitment because the football season is six months long. It's the perfect type of commitment: it suggests that you will be together for at least the next six months and leaves her looking forward to seeing you every week to watch the game.

Having a shared goal for the season is a great way to bring you two together. If you want, show her how serious you are about being together: put down a couple hundred dollars each.

Hum Along.

While walking together, start humming your song. Subtle is the key here—be like background music. Don't hum for long, just enough that she notices it's the song you two picked as your song. Don't have one? Maybe it's time. To be worthy of a couple in love, a song needs to be great and be chosen with great timing—you pick a song you like that's also playing at a romantic moment. Something that is new around the date you met may be preferred.

When you hum, you two should be in each other's arms, or at least hand in hand. Doesn't have to be on a dance floor either. Pick a park, the end of a movie when everyone else is leaving the theater, or at home.

GO FROM CASUAL TO COMMITTED

A Story from Matt

I was in the park when I began humming our song. The woman who is now my wife looked at me and said, "What are you doing?" I said, "What? I don't know what you're talking about." I knew exactly what I was doing. She looked at me with an odd expression and then held my hand for the remainder of the walk. Every once in a while, I hummed a little more.

Being sweet and acting naïve is a subtle way to flirt with your woman. Remember romance is about variety and balancing the attributes most people use to define you. If you are a guy that is bold and a bit in your face, doing something like this is a good way to show her another side most people don't get to experience.

READ A BOOK...AND THEN DISCUSS.

Did you know that the brain is our biggest sex organ? You could go with Hardy Boys or Harry Potter, but maybe something like *Men Are from Mars, Women Are from Venus* or *The Five Love Languages* may be the more enlightening choice. Pick something that she can relate to or that she wants you to relate to.

PRACTICE SPEAKING TELEPATHICALLY.

It still blows us both away to get a text from a girl at the same time we're thinking hard about her. It's like your brainwaves connect when you become lovers. Find that connection. And what astounds you will bind you together.

Take a Trip to the Store Together for a Baking Night.

The idea is to get her used to cooking for you. Just kidding—that's probably not going to happen. Since we are not pros in the kitchen, keep it simple with something you can make that is a little messy and not very complicated and tastes good. Two words: cookie dough. (The back of the chocolate chip bag will have a recipe.) Do not deny that it is a little bit great.

Make that greatness in your own kitchen with your scantily clad girl—or not so scantily clad lady, either way. There's all kind of fun things to touch and taste when you're baking cookies. Soft flour, sweet chocolate, gooey dough. Makes your senses more alive for a fun night inside. While you two are stirring and adding ingredients, be sure to take a step back and let her lead, or if she is taking a step back, be sure to step up and direct the baking party. Learn her body language, and your synergy as a couple will improve. This is where you get to be Patrick Swayze and put your hands over hers in directing what to do.

Cooking together will be a great memory for her, and memories are what build our relationships, and you may get some dessert when everything is done.

Celebrate Sweetest Day or Valentine's Day—but don't pay for both.

If you celebrate both, and we don't know why you would, then you need to come to a decision as a couple about who will get which holiday. Tell her you will make Valentine's Day special, and Sweetest Day is her day to do the same (or vice versa). Let her romance you, and don't drink too much, so you can finish the night with some lovemaking.

- As for you, here are some ideas for spending the day together:
- Shop for clothes.
- Enjoy a spa day for two.
- Make reservations for a romantic dinner.
- Give her a simple card saying how you feel about her.
- Go shopping for sex toys.
- Go to a fun event at your favorite bar or the bar where you met.
- Have a picnic at the park. Stop at a flower store for a bundle of flower petals for eight bucks and spread them around the blanket.

Just choose something and enjoy together. If you've been paying attention, you know what she likes.

LET HER SEE HOW GOOD YOU ARE WITH KIDS.

This drives women wild, so you better mean it. If you're not good with kids, learn how to be. Actually, if you are not good with kids, you should not even attempt this. Maybe go to a dog park and show her how good you are with dogs first. Baby-step this. Then you can bring the nieces and nephews around and have fun with them. You probably have not seen them enough anyway, so get two birds with one stone here.

INVITE HER OUT TO A GUYS' NIGHT.

Make sure your friends approve before and make sure it's not one of the regular places you as a group go. You want to keep your routines yours. Having quality time with your friends is important, and if one of your friends is really looking forward to that, you gotta respect it. But if they're cool with it, she will be delighted that you trust her enough to show her how you are with your friends. She'll also appreciate getting to know them a little more and seeing you in a social setting that you have created. This is another example of a controlled setting. And she may just have fun—your crew is pretty great, after all.

Take Her to Breakfast.

Saturdays are great for breakfast or brunch but are often much busier than during the week. Make reservations, or if you can't, plan to wait by getting a coffee to go and taking a stroll through the neighborhood. There is another tip earlier in this book about taking a walk to nowhere, so this could be a mini-date like that.

Back at the restaurant, it is perfectly acceptable to pop champagne before noon and pour it into your orange juice. Brunch is your girl's favorite weekend treat. Nothing makes them happier than a table in the sun, a mimosa or rosé, and some French toast. Give it a shot—you won't be sorry.

Stay Home, Get Sloppy Drunk, and Make Love.

You, her, music, and a bottle of wine or something stronger...You really can't go wrong. Play a silly drinking game, just you two. Try to do so without turning on the TV. If you do end up turning on the screen, you may end up zoning out all night and not doing what you really wanted to do. You can do quarters (flip the coin into the shot glass) for clothes or your favorite card game—you get the picture. One more tip: change from the wine to something you can do shots of.

MEDITATE TOGETHER.

Clearing your thoughts and being mindful is a great tactic for maintaining balance in life. Being present and mindful with your partner allows you two to respect the inner health you both make an effort to maintain. Mutual appreciation is furthered.

(Explain how)

MAKE A HOME PORNO.

This is going to require trust...and a tripod. And it really needs to be just for the two of you. Don't save it. Erase after watching it once. Hey, you'll be fine—if you love doing it, you will get to repeat the process!

You'll want to communicate with her about this well before you do it. What does she think of the idea? What excites her about it? What does she fear? What are your goals with it?

Prepare the room together. You may not want to go all out for the first time and rent a studio—her home or yours is fine. Where do you want to do this, and what kind of lighting or other decoration do you want to have? Figure out what kind of camera you want to use—a cell phone could be the best way to play.

GO FROM CASUAL TO COMMITTED

You may even want to prepare the "script" together—we don't mean that you have to have dialogue and a "story," like some pornos have. But maybe you two only want to be positioned a certain way, and then once that's done, turn the camera off—at least for the first home porno. Outfits are cool for some too.

The movie will be hot, but no doubt both of you will see things you're not crazy about. You may notice your stomach or that you should lean on your elbow instead of smooshing her. Once you see your O-face on video, you may change your expression out of sheer embarrassment. (Matt: I know I did!) So, make sure you share a lot of affirmations while you watch the movie, and also in the moments and even days following. You don't want to do all that and then be sad or angry about the results. Keep the negativity to yourself and practice your moves the next time or on your own, so you're ready for the next movie.

Make her a little care package.

Make up a little snack pack of fruit, cheese, nuts, and chocolate—and don't forget the note written on a napkin. Even "little snack bag for you, baby" is enough of a note. No one's expecting you to be Shakespeare. Let her know it's in the fridge in the morning, so she takes it with her.

She will go to work smiling and put the bag somewhere for all her co-workers to see. Now you have made the ever-important move of letting the work crew know that she is in a relationship. You need to break into that group so that when you meet them they already know you are a great guy. This stuff is the first impression of you; the first time they meet you is the second impression, or the confirmation impression.

> *A Story from Matt*
>
> *You know what? Little gestures are often the ones that prove just how in charge you are. For example, one time I went to a fancy restaurant, just me, for a little dinner and a glass of champagne. A good friend of mine happened to be there too, and he generously picked up my tab. "Matt," he said, "if I can afford the piano, I can afford the bench." If you can make the grand gestures, you can do the little ones too. That's still one of my favorite baller quotes.*

BECOME FACEBOOK OFFICIAL.

But don't get bullied into doing it. Do it because you want to. It means more that way. After she asks you, don't be too eager. Maybe even wait a couple hours before accepting the commitment online.

Once you are Facebook official, still have a little discretion about "checking in" on her wall and making public proclamations directed toward her for the world to see. At this point, you have only been together for a few months. You have to find a good balance of posting with her and about her. If you post too much, you are going to seem more like a fanboy than her man. If you don't post enough, she's going to be thinking that you're still creating an online perception to other women that you're single. When you include her on your social media the right way, it's going to make her day. And remember that becoming Facebook official doesn't give her permission to blow up your wall either. In fact, it's best to have a preemptive conversation about expectations of social media posting. Everyone has their own style and boundaries so make sure you have a chat so you are clear with each other.

Watch no TV tonight.

This one is gonna hurt...Talk the day before and discuss what she wants to do without the television on. Spend the night playing board games, chatting, cooking together, and enjoying whatever happens later—those are just a few options. By paying attention to one another all evening, feelings will ignite. A whole night of her not fighting the TV for your attention. Imagine how she will appreciate this...

> *A Story from Matt*
>
> *The last time I did this, I could see my wife's excitement when she walked in the door. I played music and made cocktails, and we started the evening simply discussing our day. Soon it turned into laughing and joking, then some light couch wrestling...You get the picture. Even if you don't end up in the bedroom, it's uninterrupted time together, and it strengthens the relationship.*

BUY A PUPPY TOGETHER.

...Better yet, buy a cactus. Buying a dog is a large responsibility. Getting a dog together may seem like a good idea, but it just isn't. Save that move for when you have already done the big commitment and have kids.

Okay, okay, we know you really want a dog. Don't tell us we didn't warn you. But, alright, the way to go about it is to make a big deal about it in conversation: go on and on about how you would never get a dog, and it's too much responsibility. She will argue with you just to argue, and a few months later, you can give in and get the dog together. In this way, you both get to show dominance.

A Story from Spencer

After several months of dating, my girlfriend started pushing for us to get a dog together. I was completely against the idea, but she kept pushing. Once day we were driving down Lake Shore Drive in Chicago when we saw a little dog dart across the highway. We pulled over to the side of the road, and I got out and chased the dog. This little five-pound fur ball started to run toward the lake. After about a half-mile, I finally cornered the dog. She (as I'd come to learn) had to make a choice between coming with me and jumping the eight-foot drop into massive Lake Michigan. I was certain that the dog would let me pick her up instead of jumping in the water like Harrison Ford in The Fugitive.

I was wrong. The dog jumped in and started swimming to Michigan. Despite being a poor swimmer and not knowing how I would get back up the retention wall of the lake, I jumped in and swam after the dog. I eventually caught up and brought her back to shore.

It took me a while to walk back to the car, but when I got back, my girl instantly fell in love with the dog. We put ads out to see if we could find the owner, but no one claimed her. So, basically, I was forced into a situation where my girlfriend and I had a dog together, and the story of how we saved her brought us closer together. Between the heroism of jumping in the ice-cold lake and the shared experience of nursing the dog back to health, we projected that we were the type of couple who would make good parents.

You always have to be seeding for the future. Do things today that give her in insight who you will be in the future. Lots of guys are great at talking and making promises but few know how to demonstrate their character so strongly that they don't need to make promises. I took an opportunity of almost hitting a dog on the highway to demonstrate that I'm courageous and caring. She's thinking "if he'll do that for a dog that isn't even his, imagine how he will treat me and our children." Also don't forget all of the reinforcements she will get from her girlfriends and family when she tells your heroic tale. In fact, the local newspaper did a story on this story! A little bit of fame from the article had friends of hers hitting her up, letting her know how great of a guy she landed.

SPEND SOME ALONE TIME WITH HER FAMILY

Ready to be super serious with this girl? If you are, then you have to put some time in with her family. She'd better be the one if you start down this path. Show her you're serious by spending time with the first man in her life. This will show both her and her dad that your intentions are to be a part of her family.

CHANGE YOUR NAME IN HER CONTACTS TO SOMETHING SEXY.

This may seem like a silly little idea—and it is—but it can also lead to some big revelations.

> *A Story from Matt*
>
> *I have used this two ways—one worked, and one very much did not.*
>
> *The cute way had her smiling even when I was not around. I changed my name to Studmuffin or Hotstuff, so when I texted or called, it came up like that.*
>
> *Side note:*

> *I have also used it to see if my girl was texting her ex. I saw what her ex's phone name was, changed mine to the same, and then texted her. It didn't work out well because she was still being cool with her ex even though she was texting me. That's when I had to have a serious talk with her about going all in on our relationship. I was locking her down. She needed to take it seriously, or we needed to part ways. She broke all contact with him and whoever else she was with. Her demeanor changed, and it changed for the good. This was a real turning point for her. She had a man who was standing up to her, telling her to make a decision on who she was going to be moving forward with in her life.*
>
> *Don't be a push over. This doesn't mean you should try to take control over her actions. This was more so taking a stand for the relationship. Instead of trying to control her I used this situation to let her know where I stood in the relationship. When you handle tough situations like a true gentleman, you can turn situations that have potential for destruction and turn it into a deeper connection.*

CUDDLE NAKED.

…And keep it to a cuddle. Seriously. Don't go in for major foreplay. We're not saying to do this every time but, like, every seventh time. It will drive her wild and cause all kinds of thoughts to pop into her head. This type of self-control is going to pay off in a big way down the road. Every other guy can't resist himself and constantly mauls his girl, so be different and just cuddle. Now, if she is looking for a little more than cuddling…by all means, follow her lead. You can always practice self-control the next time—and practicing that is important. She's going to assume that you'll be up for sex whenever she is, so maintain an even amount of discipline in your relationship by saying no sometimes.

Put a Picture of You Two on Your Work Desk.

Do you know how she knows you really like her? No, not by what you say to her but by what you say to others about her, and about you as a couple. Have you ever introduced the girl you're seeing as your friend or, worse, just by her name? How does the rest of your evening go after you two are alone again?

You've got to publicly show you have a girlfriend even in private settings. One simple, but majorly impressive, way to do this is to put a photo of the two of you on your desk. Then take a selfie at your desk, making sure that photo is in the background, and send it to her. It's kind of intense that women notice things in the background of pictures but useful for situations like this. To make your plan less obvious, only have half the picture in your selfie shot…her half, of course. She likely won't mention what she notices to you, but she'll mention it to her friends. Because you have given her a public place of importance at your work, you'll win points with your girl and with the people she confides in.

You've got to have a picture of you two before you can take a selfie with it, so put some thought into that first. Yes, you know how to take a photo, but just take a breath and do this one really right.

GO FROM CASUAL TO COMMITTED

Plan spontaneity. That's right, plan it. The next time you guys do something fun, plan to take a special photo. This means having your phone with a camera ready for action.

- Consider your surroundings wisely. Even if your number one activity together is hanging with your friends at the bar, a red-eyed group shot that you can crop to show just you two is not the look you're going for. Take your photo the next time you go for a walk, cook dinner in, or yes, go to the bar—but when you're there playing pool on a Sunday afternoon, just the two of you. If it's the bar where you met, then maybe take a shot of the two of you somewhere with the name visible.

- Be silly or sweet. Get out of your head and take a good shot. I know you're planning this, but try to just act natural. And it's okay if you are not usually the one taking pictures. What's she going to be suspicious of? That you are so into her that you're actually moved to do something awesome like take a picture?

- Pick the right photo. You know what, ask another woman for help if you need to—your friend, your coworker, even one of your girl's friends. You know your girlfriend is gorgeous, but she sees every blemish, shadow, and line. Make sure you pick the photo that lets her shine. You shouldn't look terrible in it, but it's okay if you look a little goofy. She'll think that's cute—and you're not the focus of this anyway. That doesn't mean you shouldn't practice first. You should take a dozen to see what is your best angle. She already knows what hers is. When you find out, remember that when taking future photos.

- Pick the right frame. What kind of frames does she have on pictures at her place? Choose one that looks like those. Or just get the mid-priced regular frame a guy would buy. Don't buy the frame that looks temporary. Think about that for a minute. If the photo is in a frame that looks like a throwaway, it gives the impression that the relationship is too. Cheap can suggest a lack of investment.

GO FROM CASUAL TO COMMITTED

A Story from Matt

This photo idea also comes in handy in gauging her thoughts on the relationship. I applied this tip in one of my relationships. I went to see the woman I was dating at her work and brought a framed photo of the two of us with me. I put it on her desk before leaving. I didn't do it in a sneaky way—just showed her the present and put it where I thought she could see it best on her desk. A couple weeks later, I went to see her at work again. There was no photo on her desk. That told me she was at a different level of investment, and I had to uncover the reason for her hesitation.

She was at work, so this was a great time to show patience and wait to have the conversation. This also allowed me to discuss without all the emotions I felt when I first noticed my symbol of love missing, despite all the effort I put into getting it there.

> *There was no clever trick for uncovering my woman's why. This was where communication came in. I had to talk with her. I made sure we were somewhere quiet and comfortable, where neither of us were likely to be distracted. I didn't make it all serious, but was thoughtful. The point was not the photo but the relationship. The photo's disappearance just gave me a reason to check in. So, I didn't dwell in judgment or accusation. She may have had to move the photo because she had a meeting in her office that required desk space, or her boss may have not allowed personal items on desks. Turns out she went back to seeing her ex and was trying to hold onto both of us. Since she wasn't serious about us we just kept it casual.*

For Christmas, drive to a neighborhood with lots of lights.

Look, we're not saying go out of your way here. You can even hit a neighborhood on the way to the grocery store. Turning off the straight path and taking a detour is the cool guy's thing to do, so make her night and check out some lights. Be sure to have already checked them out before you take her, so you don't go down a dead street.

> *A Story from Matt*
>
> *An uncle of mine took his current wife through neighborhoods to look at Christmas lights one year, and they it enjoyed it so much that even after the holidays, they just drive through neighborhoods and talk about which houses they liked best. Now during holiday season, as a married couple with a beautiful home, they still spend some of their date nights and certainly every Christmas doing the exact same thing. A simple tour of twinkling lights can turn into an anticipated tradition.*

Creating traditions that the two of you created together creates a bubble of "us". These should be things that you haven't done with any other woman. That what's makes it special. It also gives her a sense of stability. Once you claim it to be a "tradition" it indirectly demonstrates that you plan to be together for a long time.

WAVE TO HER ON FACEBOOK.

At some point, that may not be a thing to do anymore. (Already when we were writing this, it wasn't much of a thing.) So, what we mean by this is, do something silly online. Poke her, like her photo, or share her tweet. It's cute in a silly type of way, and it's supportive of her online persona. Just don't become her fan instead of her boyfriend — you're not just any old person commenting on her profile, so talk like her boyfriend. And please do not "piss" all over her page, marking your territory, so everyone knows you're her boyfriend. If an online conversation gets heated, have her back but don't fight her fights. Don't drop declarations of love all over the place either. That is so annoying to everyone, especially her.

Start the New Year Right and End It Right.

On New Year's Eve, you better be standing next to her for that midnight kiss.

On New Year's Day, bust out some Bloody Mary mix and start the day with a cocktail, together. Even if it's a virgin drink, you can still make a Bloody Mary that looks like the real thing.

This is where you plan ahead and show you can plan for the future. Before the stores close and you go out for the night on December 31, pick up some Bloody Mary mix, vodka (if you want), celery, olives, and pickled veggies—not for that night but for the next day. Nobody wants to be running out of the house with a hangover on January 1, looking for a place that's open.

Learn the Names of her Extended Family.

This goes along with the idea that you take her seriously and want to learn about her family. Being able to address her aunts and uncles by name will show her you plan to be seeing them over time. Plus, it's just polite.

It also makes her more committed in the relationship because now the family is going to accept you a little. This doesn't lock you in by any means, but it takes the heat off you; you're no longer an unknown guy she is dating.

Go fly a kite.

Yes, that's a real thing! You can actually still buy kites and fly them on gorgeous days down by the water or out in a field.

Practice before you go with her if you don't know how. Your reputation as an athlete is on the line. I'm not saying it's hard, but it's not easy, so try it once before you have an audience. This is going to be a memory you get to talk to your kids about when you take them, so practicing is highly recommended.

Pack a picnic before you go to extend the outing. Okay, okay. At least bring a couple bottles of water or ask her to pack a picnic, and you bring the kite as a surprise. This would be a good spot for a picture of the two of you, kite in hand at a park.

PLAY TOURIST.

Staycation, baby! A weekend, including a night in a hotel, or a day, or even your lunch break will work. How often do you go to your city's main tourist attractions? Have you ever gone? When you see something every day, you forget about it. Worse, sometimes you start to think of it as just for tourists. But this is your home! These are your attractions! Go get 'em! You don't need to get a flight or hotel room, unless you don't want to stay at your house. Explore your town like a tourist and take your woman with you. Could be funny to even dress like a tourist.

Borrow or rent a couple bikes.

If you don't already bike together, now's your time. Friends will have bikes you can borrow, or rent them at a bike shop or even hotel. We don't know a girl who wouldn't want to do this. It's innocent fun that has you two spending quality time together.

There are some amazing bike trails now. Oh, and don't imagine you are going to do an all-day bike ride. If you don't bike regularly, keep it to under a couple hours, for your butts' sakes. Then again, you can always give one another butt massages when you get back!

Text her all day about all the dirty things you're going to do when you see her next.

When you get home, don't just go right into it. Let her body language tell you what's up. If she is lighting candles and rushing through dinner to get to bed early, this could be a good sign. Either way, be sure to make some moves and start with reminding her in soft whispers through the evening about all the tasty things you said you were going to do to her. Remind her about one thing while you're at dinner, another while you're cleaning up…You get the picture.

When Times Get Tough Set Boundaries and Give Her the Space to Leave.

Every woman is going to push the line to see where your boundaries are. As a man, you have to know where your personal boundaries are and enforce them in a way that is stern but still respectful.

In this part of the relationship, she might want to accelerate things and want to move in together, get a puppy, or start going on elaborate vacations together. You don't want the relationship to escalate too quickly. You have to stick to your principles and enforce them. As long as your principles are made with good intention, you shouldn't budge. Even if that means she leaves you.

For example, if she wants to move in together at this point, you have to say no. She may fight you on this. She might say, "I'm at your place every day, and I already have a lot of my stuff here. I don't see why we just can't move in together." She might try to convince you with sex, she might try to build a logical case, or she might threaten to leave you. Women will continue to push until they find out where the line is. Once they find the line, the way you handle it will set the tone for the entire course of your relationship.

There may come a point when she says, "If you don't want to move in together, then I'm not sure if I want to be with you anymore." This usually causes men to instantly give in or to get really defensive and say, "Well, if you don't like it, then there's the door."

You have to play it somewhere in the middle. Tell her that she always has the option to leave and that you would never do anything to control her. Then state that you've made a decision that you are absolutely not going to move in together right now, so if that is necessary for her to be in this relationship, then you'll accept that.

If she's emotional, she might twist your words to make it appear as if you are breaking up with her, so you need to be very clear. Tell her something like this: "I want to be with you, but I feel very strongly that it isn't wise for us to move in together. I want to give this relationship the chance to be something long-term and stable, so I feel it's best to take things slow. I'm not moving in with you, but I'm also not leaving you. If you want to leave because I'm sticking to my principles, I'll be sad, but I will certainly understand. If this is a deal breaker, then I understand, although I don't like it, but you should also stick to *your* principles."

In our experience, nine times out of ten, she won't leave. In fact, women usually become more attracted to men when they realize that they know how to make tough decisions based on a strong belief in their principles. That's the type of man a woman wants to attach herself to. A man who is compassionate but firm. A man who thinks before he acts and is unwilling to be pushed around even if it's by the thing he loves the most. A woman might not like it when she's on the other side of it, but she will love it when those attributes are on her side and working for her.

This can apply to any disagreement you may have. Be flexible when the issue is nominal but be unwilling to budge when you really believe in your decision.

GO FROM CASUAL TO COMMITTED

A Story from Matt

One time, I had just lost my job but actually felt pretty good about it. They gave me a good severance package, and I decided to take the summer off. I had met an amazing girl and wanted the time I normally wouldn't have to get serious with her. My girlfriend at the time wasn't so into it, though, and told me she needed her space. She was clearly blowing me off so she didn't have to deal with my personal issues. I said I didn't have issues, but if that was the kind of person she was—the kind who would leave me when she thought I was down, I was glad to know that sooner than later. Well, it really shook her up, and boy, did her actions show how much she wanted to be with me after that. So I decided to see how badly she wanted to be with me. At one point, she thought I was going to meet her at a bar, but I didn't. When she texted, I nonchalantly replied where I was. Sure as shit, she brought all her friends over to where I was.

I had to be willing to walk away from her and be willing for her to walk away from me. I needed to take the risk of being single to see how bad she wanted my attention. And then if she were to choose to stay, as this girlfriend did, I needed her to come to me also for all of her friends to see how important I am to her.

> *If you do something like this and your girl chooses to walk, I have to point out this plus: all those girls you blew off when you were in a relationship will be like flies on crap when they find out you're single. Women are looking for a creative, faithful man as much as we men are looking for a woman we can trust and who won't make fun of the inner secrets we have shared.*
>
> *In other words, you can't fear putting break-up wheels in motion. When you tell your woman you want to break it off, you are in the driver's seat instead of riding bitch.*
>
> *You're being the bitch may have been one of the reasons she was drifting away. You are going to need to look at yourself and figure out what was happening and make some changes.*

DEEPEN THE CONNECTION

Months 6–9

- ✓ Be irreplaceable.
- ✓ Set expectations for her and yourself.
- ✓ Answer with brutal honesty.
- ✓ Create space in the relationship.

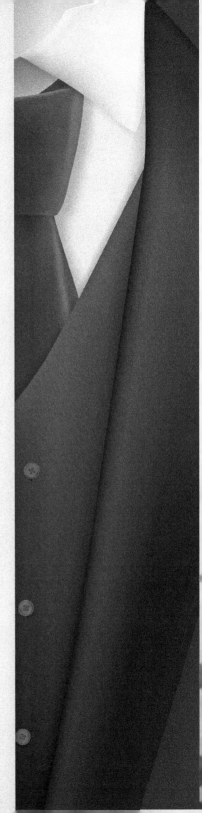

This phase is the heartbeat that expands and contracts your relationship by creating a pulse in your connection together, emotionally and physically. To seal the connection of the relationship, you must draw her in closer and become irreplaceable. So close together you don't need words. The next beat expands the relationship by creating distance, which tests the limits and reveals your boundaries. This creates additional layers of trust as she realizes that the rings will never break even when the relationship feels weakened.

Once your lives are integrated and you've fallen into well-defined roles as lovers and partners, it's time again to turn up the heat and magnify her love until her passion is a healthy balance between freedom and obsession. When you are done with this phase, she will be convinced that there is no other man on the planet that could come close to being a better suitor.

The key to this phase is about making yourself indispensable in her eyes, while simultaneously making her a better lover and partner for you. You make yourself indispensable by demonstrating that you know how to please her in the specific ways that only a man deeply rooted in her soul could. You anticipated her needs and desires while opening her up to experiences she didn't even know she wanted.

The more you can anticipate her needs, the more permission you have to be bold in stating yours. Most men will serve a woman's needs with the hopes that she will reciprocate.

The reality is that many women usually are natural givers or naturally selfish, so understand that you have to lead her to treat you the specific ways you like to be treated.

Great relationships are ones that have well-defined expectations. Simply stating what you want isn't enough. There must be both positive and negative reinforcements, so you and your partner clearly know where the lines are drawn. It's your job to guide the ups and downs of the relationship to shape the clear expectations you have of each other.

Holding your woman to certain expectations and having her tell you her expectations makes you both better partners. This isn't accomplished by bossing her around and punishing her when she doesn't perform but rather through guiding her by clearly stating what you want her to do and bringing some type of playful energy to it. Punishment is a penalty for unacceptable behavior. It's a natural part of life but using punishment to control the relationship is temporary and abusive.

There are moments in the relationship when you have to

address negative behavior. She may also punish you for doing something stupid, but you two are in this for the long haul, so once the behavior is corrected, you then guide the relationship by getting to the root of the action that caused the problem.

Tips

CALL HER AND TALK DIRTY.

Ahh, good ol' dirty talk. Step one in the non-tangible arousal department. You pick up the phone for a light evening chat, and suddenly your partner is using words to light your body on fire. You thought it was just a check-in—now your minds are racing for the hottest next move. Desire is a great way to keep the relationship alive. Use it to your advantage.

Talking dirty is an art, but nowadays you can get help. Find your favorite sultry website, and you can read sexy nothings into her ear. Don't stop even if she is uncertain about reciprocating. Let her know you will do all of the talking.

DEEPEN THE CONNECTION

A Story from Matt

I had a girlfriend who wasn't the best at responding, but she'd tell me which stories made her hot, which worked out well because I knew more of what to try when I saw her in person. I would even study more of the dirty-forum stories that had the subject "getting her hot," so I could use the words with her or read her the story as foreplay when we were together. This worked out well for me because my mouth was busy, so she had to use hers.

Woman want a man that can seemingly read her mind. Most of the time we bitch about this because it seems like an unrealistic expectation, but if you know how to access her imagination you can figure out what makes her tick. Women don't want to tell you what they like, they want you to figure it out. So take the time to dig a little deeper and show her that you can read between the lines of what she says... and what she's NOT saying. Put in a little effort and it will be seem like you can actually read her mind and anticipate her fantasies.

Go forty-eight hours without speaking to, texting, or seeing each other.

Embrace the pain of missing her. It's tough but a great way to build up the excitement of seeing one another, and it's also a nice breather. If you are happier in that forty-eight hours than you are usually, you may want to consider another forty-eight hours, and then, if still happier without her it may be time to just move on. No need to waste your time if she isn't the right girl. All of these tips are meant to keep the girl who's right for you. During a regular period, see if you can go without having to text her every three hours. Does she text you, or is she silent? Who knows—maybe you are the one holding the relationship up and it will only last as long as you care to hold it upright. Better to find out now.

Take genuine interest in a show she loves that you hate.

The Kardashians or the Real Housewives may suck or not be, in your eyes, a guy thing to watch, but she loves it, so sit with her and enjoy her while she enjoys the show. Just remember not to join in on conversations at work when it comes up or you are going to be found out.

Get her favorite candy.

Get her favorite candy and make her "trick or treat." The idea is to make her beg for the candy...but you are doing it in a cute way, so it's okay. Why make her beg for it? It's playful and sometimes it's fun to tease each other. Do you know what her favorite candy is? Well, maybe you should ask, and not the day of Halloween either. Ask when you're both in the grocery store about a month before the holiday but don't buy it then.

When she has something on her face, tell her...and learn to love her flaws.

This is not really romantic, but it's rude when you don't. This is also a good way to start building trust. It demonstrates that you are willing to be honest with her even if she might be embarrassed a little bit. As your relationship progresses, she'll actually believe it when you say she doesn't look fat in that dress and pull the loose hair off her jacket sleeve and stuff like that. She has to know you have her back and, well, her front.

Learn To Love her Flaws

A Story from Spencer

Here's a funny extreme example of this. I was dating this girl who had a little skin tag right on her neck—right on the kissable part, as it would turn out. Now, I'm the kind of guy who picks scabs, so that tag drove me nuts. I wasn't sure how it had hung on for as long as it had; it was connected to her by just a thread. I couldn't stand it, but I couldn't say anything yet, as it was early in the relationship. Then, one night while we were making out, I thought, "I'm going to go for it," and I just bit it right off. That's how I ended up getting rid of it—I just snapped it right off with my teeth. She jumped a little, but that was it. Needless to say it didn't work out because I didn't accept her the way she was. I didn't love her flaws.

DEEPEN THE CONNECTION

> *My parents went to couple's counseling once, and one of the things I remember that counselor telling them was if your husband or wife has a mole, and you don't like it from the beginning, over time, you're going to grow to hate it, and then you're going to grow to hate the person. You have to know right now what your choice is going to be: do you hate that mole or love it, or can you do something about it? It's not about the crusty sleep in the eyes or the skin tag or the mole—it's about the way you deal with it, and you have to, not only out of politeness, sometimes, but for the sake of your relationship. That skin tag came off but if she were the one and it was a birthmark or something like that I would learn to love it as so should you.*
>
> *At the end of the day you have to decide if you can love ALL of her. The good, the bad, the weird and everything in-between. When you commit to a woman you're committing to every bit of her. I've found out that the minor perceived flaws of woman usually end up being the endearing things you remember about her.*

COME UP BEHIND HER AND COVER HER EYES. WHISPER, "GUESS WHO?"

When she guesses your name, whisper, "No, your man-candy."

You can sub out "your man-candy" for anything you like—your beast, your gladiator, your champion, even your lover; just keep it sexy. It's all about getting her to think of you as your best you, her fantasy you, the sexy you.

Pro tip: Be sure to wash your hands before you do this metro stunt. (a) You're about to touch her eyes, and (b) she will be able to smell your fingers. Potato chip fingers, or worse, and it could be the story she is telling her friends tomorrow.

DEEPEN THE CONNECTION

This idea is enough in and of itself—not everything has to be a grand gesture, and you should be showing her you care in little ways throughout each day. But if you want this to be the start of something more, consider having something more at the ready.

- If you're her man-candy, once she's turned around, have a favorite sweet of hers at the ready. It can be as simple as a store-bought candy or as complicated as a dessert you've made.
- Her gladiator? You've done one of her chores that she's been putting off.
- Her champion? You know things have been rough at her work, and you're ready with a listening ear and a foot rub.
- And if you're her beast…well, stud, you know what you need to suggest to your lady…

Ask her what her favorite part of your body is.

And then set a reminder in your phone for a week or a month later to take a pic of that body part. Send it to her.

Hopefully she said your eyes...

You are establishing a couple things here. First of all, you are making a great memory and showing you can follow through. Second, you're demonstrating humor and obviously patience. She may not even remember the conversation at first, so be sure to remind her. Go ahead and say, "I remember you telling me about your favorite..."

Ask her to make your favorite meal. Do the dishes afterward.

Most women are natural caretakers and love to nurture, especially when they feel loved. Asking her to make your favorite meal is something that lets her care for you. Cleaning up afterward shows your appreciation for her.

Start out with the conversation of what her favorite thing to cook is. If she says nothing, run! No, no. Just kidding. In that case, you just have a little more work to do, and her cooking for you may be you two cooking together.

Once she has told you her favorite dinner recipe, you have to try it. Don't ask but suggest to her when to make it. You choose the day, and she can choose if she wants to cook at your house or hers. If you live together, then she can pick the time.

DON'T LET HER TANTRUM TURN INTO A FIGHT.

When you're arguing, she might start getting emotional and start throwing a fit. She's not nagging you and giving you attitude because she's genuinely mad. She's giving you attitude because she is emotional and wants to have a conversation about it. The key is to allow her to throw a tantrum; do not push back.

She is going to push your buttons, and you are going to want to defend yourself, but don't. Remember, when you do, you are feeding the beast. Let her have her say and then give it some time. Once she has calmed down, you can let her know you are ready to talk about it.

DEEPEN THE CONNECTION

Set an expectation for communication. Say to her, "Don't tell me that you don't feel something—tell me what you actually feel." If she continues to argue with you in a vague way, if she just wants to launch at you, say, "I'm going to end this conversation now, and we can have it when you're ready to talk like a big girl." That'll push her buttons like nothing else does, but you have to hold your ground. What you're saying to her is "I'm not leaving you; I'm just going to remove myself from this." This isn't the only way or the way to react every time, of course, but it's an example.

Just like a child, she will give you attitude *because* she wants you to push back. Don't fall into the trap. Sometimes allowance is the best discipline. The first few times this is going to get her right back to yelling or having a fit, but if you keep calm and don't react, you will be able to change the way you both communicate.

Pick out her outfit.

Leave it on her bed with a note of where and when to meet you. Make sure it's someplace nice, though. She isn't going to get all dressed up to go to Arby's. That dress she wore on your first date. Good choice. That little black number she wore to that event when you couldn't stop staring at her. Also good. The smile that she will be wearing when she sees that you chose her outfit for the evening that you planned all by yourself as a surprise. Priceless.

DEEPEN THE CONNECTION

GIVE HER A GIFT CARD TO VICTORIA'S SECRET AND TELL HER YOUR FAVORITE COLOR.

Sometimes less is more. Lingerie shopping is one of those times, if you know what we mean.

You are telling her your favorite color and type of lingerie you like to be the director here. This is a little bit of a control scenario. Men need to be in control, and women like men to be in control, or at least let the man feel he is in control sometimes, and this is one of those times. She'll be wearing the item, but in her eyes, it's really something for you, so you should communicate what you want. Favorite color, favorite style, or favorite fabric. Include if you like lace, string straps, no bra, stockings, corsets—share it all. You can't be shy or bashful when it comes to this. A woman wants a man who knows what he wants, so be detailed and don't be bashful. She will do as you ask.

HAVE HER BUY YOU SOME SOCKS.

Wear socks that have some holes in them and make sure your girl sees them. When your lady mentions the holes, you can ask her to get you some new ones. If you don't ask, she may not do it, and with this tactic, you're practicing showing her you can ask for what you want.

You can ask her to do any specific little task for you. Say you're making out with a girl who is wearing peppermint lip balm. (You'll want to—that stuff is crazy amazing. It's like having one of those hotel mints in your mouth the whole time.) Ask her to buy you a tube of it. She might have to go to three or four stores to find it. Getting her to buy you something is getting her to invest in you.

DEEPEN THE CONNECTION

A Story from Matt

My mother always said, if she's not going to instinctively and without prompting buy you socks and underwear and the right pants for your work, she's not for you. A real woman will make sure her man has his essentials, always.

Mom is right—your woman should be mothering you. You're going to daddy her once in a while. Anyway, it's not really mothering as much as it is looking out for you and making sure you look your best when you go to work.

Deep down we are looking for a partner that resembles how our parents loved us. If this goes too far you can start to become codependent. The key is to appreciate it without being needy for it. At the end of the day you are an independent man but it's nice to be babied sometimes.

SUPPORT GIRLS' NIGHT OUT.

When your girlfriend informs you that she has a girls' night planned, call the restaurant and order a round of drinks to her table—if you're a real baller, a bottle of nice champagne. Be sure to remember what your lady is wearing before she leaves because you will need to describe what she looks like to the host. Better yet, ask for the manager. If your girl is hot, the manager may just send over the drinks on the house, but you get all the credit with her and her friends.

Not only will you receive a text from your lady but you will also get a few from her friends that night. Establishing good rapport with your lady's group is important for a couple reasons. If she's a social person, you want her to remember that just because she is having her own time doesn't mean you don't care (and remind her, as she parties the night away, that she has a boyfriend who cares about her). And all those people behind the scenes—parents, friends, family—are either going to advocate for you or they're going to destroy your relationship from the outside.

Play grab ass.

Grab her butt as you pass by her in the house. Wink and smile when she turns around. You are reminding her that she is sexy and that she turns you on. A pinch here and a grab there is good for both people in a relationship. I'm not saying to pull a Trump and "grab her by the pussy", but sexy grabs and touches make for a healthy relationship.

Ask her to pick out your shirt for tomorrow.

Let's face it—you don't really care what you wear, and she will think the task is cute. Don't act like you need help, though. Act like you want her expert clothing advice. So, you may ask, why do you want to do this? Simple: you're including her in your life, and it also gives you free smiles every time you see yourself in the shirt that she picked for you.

DEEPEN THE CONNECTION

A Story from Spencer

I once dated a woman that was a stylist. She was always on me to be "camera ready" even when we were at home just scrubbing it. Since she was so passionate about this I allowed her to pick out my outfit every day. She loved it! She would end each night mindfully looking at my closet to decide what outfit would represent me best for the next day. This ended up talking at the end of the night about what I had going on the next day. So not only did she feel good serving me with her gift but it opened up the conversation to what we had going on the next day and what our goals were.

Now if this isn't something your lady is into, don't push it upon her to dress you. That make you look like a child but if this is a way for her to lovingly support you, allow it. She might be into cooking or planning vacations, decorating the house or taking care of your health. Whatever it is, let her take the lead and some responsibilities off your plate.

GIVE HER AN HONEST *AND* CONSTRUCTIVE ANSWER WHEN SHE ASKS HOW SHE LOOKS IN THAT DRESS.

If you're not too much of a dick, she'll appreciate it. Be sure to start with a positive (like how it makes her chest look), followed by the truth (give it to her straight about how it fits over her butt), and then add another compliment (like the color). Now that you may have pissed her off a little, you have to offer a solution. Say, "Let me help you choose something"—how about that black dress you like?

Think of this tip as an 80/20 rule: compliment your woman 80 percent of the time, but feel free the other times to let her know that you really don't like what's happening with her clothes or hair or whatever. Doing so is good because it's honest, and it also makes your compliments worth something—you're saying that when you give compliments, you mean them, because you're not afraid to criticize.

When she asks what you think about the outfit she has on, she really isn't looking for fashion advice. What she's really asking is "Do you want to bang me in this dress?" So, give her a response that reflects your answer.

Ask her how much she loves you... then ask her why.

Now, don't let her off the hook when she doesn't answer the question or does it in a general way. Ask her again if she loves you. It's good to get her to think about the reasons why she is with you. Do it with a smile and keep it light but keep asking her till she gives you an answer. The sincere reply will come out once you show her you are not letting her off the hook.

When you get into a fight about something stupid and apologize, make it up to her right away.

Let her win this one. She will see you are reasonable and thoughtful, and you won't have "sold out" because it was something you don't care about.

A Story from Matt

I have started quite a few arguments and had so much passion behind them that I would never back down simply for ego's sake, but I remember starting an argument about pizza for a party that my girlfriend had planned. I basically came in and started changing things at the last minute, knowing this would get her goat. I also wanted to show I was flexible in an argument, so I insisted that we order delivery pizza instead of buying pizzas from the grocery store. She flipped and said absolutely not and that she would never spend that kind of money and wanted to show her guests a great time with timed and fresh pizza from the oven. I barely pushed back but then gave in; if it were something I really cared about, I certainly would not have given even an inch. I apologized for trying to change her plans. I then volunteered to cook the pizzas, so she could be the hostess, which was great for me, 'cause it gave me something to do. She couldn't have been happier, especially since she hardly ever won arguments with me.

DEEPEN THE CONNECTION

A Story from Spencer

Here's a great example that happened to a friend of mine.

He and his girlfriend were updating their kitchen, and she had all these catalogs about drawer handles and paint colors. He didn't care about any of that stuff, but he acted like he did. She wasn't expecting the pushback and got kinda mad at facing his resistance at every turn. My buddy really worked this—he held on from lunchtime one Saturday all the way to dinner. And then he took them out to dinner at the place she'd been dying to try but that took reservations. Over dinner, relaxed by the wine and good food, his girlfriend admitted that though the day hadn't been fun, she was touched that he cared so much about the home they shared together.

If you're going to pull something like my friend did, it works best if you can anticipate when a discussion is going to happen (he knew his girlfriend would want to talk about the kitchen when they were both home from work on Saturday), so you can make a reservation early that week for a restaurant that is cool, but not so cool that it requires months for a reservation--and quiet.

Again, if you can anticipate her needs, she feels like you truly are paying attention to what she has going on in her life. Nothing makes a woman feel more loved than a man is thinking about her when she's not around.

INVITE HER MOM OVER TO THE HOUSE.

Only invite her if your girl likes her mom, of course.

You'll learn more about your lady by getting to know her mom. When you ask your girl's mom what she was like when she was her daughter's age, you are going to get a looking glass of how your girlfriend really is. Traits are passed down and amazingly similar in parents and kids. (Matt: I should know—I see my kids doing all the things I never got caught doing.)

BUY HER A GIFT TO GIVE TO HER BOSS.

Maybe it's around Christmas or maybe her team just sealed a big deal, but helping her become a success is as important as her making you a success. Be a team player. Well, only be a team player if you know what her boss would want. A Gucci tie or pocket square is always a hit for men. I also like personalized cufflinks with the boss's initials engraved. For the female boss, we would suggest tickets to the opera and not some item you see plenty of in her office.

DEEPEN THE CONNECTION

GO TO THANKSGIVING WITH HER FAMILY.

I know that you barely want to go to Thanksgiving with **your** family, much less a partner's scrutinizing family. Here's the thing to remember, though—it's probably the best holiday to choose from. There's a game on TV for entertainment; maybe the parade is still on; it's a time when everyone is grateful; and since it's the beginning of the holiday season, people tend to be on their best behavior. So, talk shop, kiss babies, and eat the turkey. Definitely don't get into debates or comment on topics like religion or politics. This is how they get you sucked in. Don't fall for it.

Your job lasts well past the meal. On the way home, the most romantic thing you can do is *not* complain about the traffic, the food, or the relatives.

HAVE HER UNDRESS FOR YOU BEFORE BEDTIME.

We love this one because she may want to do it–well, not it, but something sexy for you and is just waiting for the right time. So, create the right time! She may not go immediately into exotic dancer mode. Even the most gorgeous woman can be nervous about her body and having someone's gaze concentrated on her. Do whatever you need to make her feel comfortable. And ask her to undress one article at a time, even lingering over jewelry. This isn't about the big reveal of key areas; this is about the sexiness of her moves and the vulnerability she is sharing with you. Be thoughtful and appreciative of every part of her.

It's not saying, "Let's have sex," but it's a start. At the least, there will be hugs soon after, so enjoy.

As a part two, or if she remains hesitant to have you watch her, have her undress you instead. This offers a point of contact and affection that may otherwise not happen. Sometimes, you have to ask for it. She may tell you to do a strip tease for her, so be ready to dance. Don't try to imitate strippers. Guys strip differently than women, so have fun and be sexy-funny.

WATCH OR READ PORN TOGETHER.

Enjoy what you like privately…together! Now, you may say that this is going too far. Well, we have discovered some crazy sexual secrets this way and given away a few of our own. What a way to add an exciting edge to your sex life and connect on another level. You learn more about each other as individuals, and you both may be (delightedly) shocked by what turns the other on. This may open you both up to be more creative and ask for more on your own.

What we really love about this is that it starts an open and honest conversation about masturbating, which we all do (except those special few, and we're sure half of those special few are lying).

If she's a little unsure, suggest a field trip to the local sex-positive, women-run sex shop. (If you live in a city, there's likely one there; if you don't, or even if you do but just don't want to go there in person, shop online.) It does not have to be degrading, and those shops will have books and videos you may both be pleasantly surprised by—and totally turned on with.

If she still isn't comfortable with it, give her a *Penthouse* letters book and ask her to read privately. Then you can discuss what stories she liked the best. If you don't think she will read them, then read those stories together. That may be what opens the door to more shared exploration.

THE COOL GUY'S GUIDE

A Story from Spencer

Pornography can be a touchy subject in a relationship, but it's something nearly everybody can at least relate to. The reason we have so much shame talking about porn is because we do it behind closed doors and in secrecy. Behind your woman's metaphorical curtains are all her secret sexual desires. So, ask her what type of porn she likes to watch. In fact, ask her what was the last porn she watched. Ask her if she watched the whole thing or if she fast-forwarded it to a certain part. Not many girls get to openly share these things. Not only will you know more how to sexually please her, but she will also feel closer to you.

When I'm traveling it's hard to keep up sexual intimacy. When me and my girl are apart we share with each other our sexual fantasies through video selection. It can be more than just pornography. It can be a sexy meme or a well written Instagram post that got you a little hot. This lets each other know that anything sensual that you come across make you think about each other. When you do it in secret it can make it seem like your sexual fantasies are allowing your mind to wander to other woman. When you include her you can use your lonely sexual impulses as a way to fantasize together.

DEEPEN THE CONNECTION

Ask her to rub your feet and then return the favor.

It's maybe more common to ask for and give a foot massage than a butt massage, but it's still not as common, or as easy, as the shoulders. The shoulders you can squeeze with one hand as you clear her dinner dish with the other. The feet, though—for those, you both have to be sitting in a comfortable place (not the subway, for example), with shoes and, ideally, socks, off. But, oh man, is that a spot that earns appreciation. The feet are two of our hardest-working body parts.

We like the idea of you requesting the massage, rather than offering to give it, first. Doing things for you should be her pleasure as much as it is yours, just as the reverse is true. She will like the surprise of getting a foot rub after you've gotten one. Give that wonderful surprise to your girl. (Plus, let's face it—that way she can't back out of giving your dogs a rub. Asking for you first shows her you ask for what you want.)

If she says no or that you should massage her first, forget it. Try again another time. Don't give in here. It's not the point to just spoil her all the time. You need her to listen to your needs as much as you do hers. Let her know that.

Here are some suggestions for making this a better than average massage:

Take a shower or at least wash your feet in the sink. Brush the sock lint away. Trim your nails and have your shoes off before you ask. You don't want that stinky foot smell coming out while she is taking your shoes off. Phew.

- Have some massage oil or lotion handy.
- Put some music on and be prepared to talk with her or just gaze into her eyes while you rub. This is one of those rare massages during which you face the other person.

She may not want you to rub her feet. Some people are extremely ticklish there (or she may have a blister or something else going on down there). Well, too bad for her, but you can still do something nice and relaxing for her feet or ankles, like draw her a warm foot bath, or what about—and stick with me here—what about giving her a pedicure? Toes are easy: they have little nails, so not much to paint, and you don't need to worry about many people seeing your handiwork. Guess what—when you have kids, you are gonna have to do it with them, so you may as well learn now. Or sit down next to her, pat your lap, indicating that she should swing her legs up there, and massage her ankles, calves, shins, and knees. And, who knows…she may want you to move north of the knees.

Take her out. Buy her a dress. Bring her to a place where you two can show off.

This is another example of appearing spontaneous while actually planning. As far as she knows, you two are just going to go eat lunch. But after you eat, bring her into a nice shop and see if she likes any of the dresses. If so, then buy her one. Now, on the way home, see if she wants to wear the dress out. Then, take her out! It doesn't have to be that night, and a later date will give her that special feeling longer as she looks forward to the date and how sexy she is going to look for you. Remember, you picked it out together, so she already knows you like what she is gonna wear, which often is a huge part of the decision when girls are deciding what to wear when they go out.

By starting the day with a simple outing (say, for breakfast or lunch or a coffee while strolling in the park), which turns into a new dress for her, and then a nice night out, you just became her prince charming. Since you bought her that dress specifically for that dinner, she is forever going to remember both of them.

Treat a woman like a princess and you will be treated like royalty as well. Admiration and respect for her breeds admiration and respect for you. Going above and beyond unexpectedly, shows her how lucky she is and grows your bond.

Some girls get nervous shopping with their boyfriends when all eyes are on them. Some stores will set up a separate room for your girl, which gives her a little more privacy. If that's not in the cards, you can still buy her an outfit. It just requires a little more planning. There are great stores that have no-hassle return policies. Go, buy more than one item, bring the outfits back, and have her try them on ("Have a fashion show" is a tip that offers more details about this). Tell her you'll return whatever she doesn't want, no problem.

Suggest she take you out for ice cream.

It's nice to receive surprises, for the other person to just invite you to do what she's come up with, but it can actually be nice to ask for something too. And she'll be happy to fulfill such an easy desire!

This tactic also acts as the start of a long-term pattern. We're not saying girls are cheap, but it's easier to convince her to take you for ice cream than a steak dinner, and the idea here is to get her used to the idea of her taking care of you and chipping in on outings. It's not all your financial responsibility to bear these days.

MAKE EACH OTHER HEALTHIER.

Physical attraction is a big reason why your partner is your partner. Buying the same gym membership as your partner is a great way to encourage one another to spend time there regularly. If that's too much time together, at least have the same schedule for working out.

Another helpful tactic is to be aware of what you're buying at the grocery store. Cook healthy together. Don't leave it to her to count your caloric intake each day and schedule dinner accordingly; instead, discuss meal options together. Discuss desired health goals as well. You might as well utilize your partner for accountability.

FUEL THE FIRE

Months 9–12

- ✓ Be romantically over the top.
- ✓ Let your guard down.
- ✓ Be agreeable.
- ✓ Treat her like a queen.

The biggest challenge while putting her on a pedestal is the fear of losing your balls, but if you approach treating her like a queen as though you are a king and not a joker, then it will not emasculate you. In fact, you will both feel empowered that you are sharing the company of royalty. This is the phase where you enter "power couple" status.

This is also the phase when you let it all out. Spend more money, carve out more time, tell her things you've never told anyone else. When you properly put a woman on a pedestal, she starts to see all other men as a joke by comparison and her loyalty will be undying.

At this point in the relationship, you are the center of her universe. If you have followed all the steps, you should have a well-defined relationship with a woman who is certain that you were created specifically for her. She has proven over and over that she understands you by the way she serves you. Other people will start to comment on the way she looks at you, and her devotion is as strong as her love. Your love will also shine and you won't be able to contain the words of your devotion to her friends and family.

Once she has proven that she can constantly evolve and

continue to be devoted as well as keep the spark alive, it's time to completely let your guard down and make her feel like a queen…but *only* once she has reciprocated. This is where her competitiveness to be the top priority in your life is finally satisfied.

Tips

FANTASIZE ABOUT HER WHEN SHE'S NOT AROUND.

You have found your girl now, so stop looking left and right down the street. Look past the faces and enjoy your walk. It's time to change your mind on how you think. This is where you begin building lifelong positive inner thoughts about her.

So many of these tips are about letting your woman know what you think of her or even about letting her friends know what you think of her. But doing something that no one but you will ever know…well, that can be the most powerful action of all. All this time, you have been having the craziest fantasies with other women, so start incorporating her into them. If you can't, then there may be a bigger issue to resolve. Replace those faces with hers and get turned on by her.

She may never know that you privately fantasize about her, but she'll see how those fantasies change your attitude toward her. We all build up walls, so practice seeing her as your true soul mate. Your imaginations can lead you on a better path.

A Story from Matt

It's okay to sometimes clue her in on these thoughts. When I'm on road trips, I call my wife and tell her the thoughts I have of her and how I think of her when I am alone in my room. Then I hint at my specific thoughts. One time when I was in the mood, I told her exactly how my fantasy went. By the time I got home, we both had twinkles in our eyes and playful smirks on our faces. And pretty soon that was all we were wearing.

When you're not around, your woman knows that you still have sex on your mind. So if you aren't bringing it up periodically she may be wondering where all of that sexual energy is going. When you let her into where your mind is at during the day she's going to feel safer when you are away.

Enjoy couple's yoga.

Get in touch with each other's body and spirit. You can find a class to take together—a lot of yoga studios even offer the first class for free—or put on an internet class to work through on your own. You probably won't go to more than three or four sessions, so don't buy too many passes, but still gain the check mark for trying the things she likes.

Buy or pick some flowers for her place, put them in a vase, and leave them on a table.

This does work best if you clean the room a little—the point is to give her a little slice of perfect "home" to return to.

Don't worry about how the flowers are put in the vase; she will start rearranging them regardless.

Spend the night in, watching a movie you both loved in high school.

Make it a throwback night. Don't drink, or just drink silly things like root beer. Get corn to pop, and we're not talking about the microwavable kind—in-the-pan-type, old-school popcorn making. And stick to making out and hand stuff, just like in the old days. Think second base for the fooling around. Making out for a long time on the couch is just what you both may need to show how much in love you are and that it's not just about sex but the bond you both have with each other.

> *A Story from Spencer*
>
> *If you are traveling and you can't spend time together I've got a great tip for you. If you use the video conferencing app, Zoom, you are able to have a video chat while sharing your computer screen AND the audio from the computer. This allows you to watch a movie together while still being able to see each other and talk. My girl and I do this so we can feel like we are at the movies together or like we are sitting in the living room watching our favorite show.*

It's important to make her feel like you are there even when you're not. If you really want to step up your game use the Postmates app and order her favorite candy and wine. There is no reason that you can't serve here even though you're not there. When you do simple things like this, it gives you more freedom to spend time conquering the world while traveling because you are making an effort to stay connected.

GO SEE A CHICK FLICK INSTEAD OF THE ACTION-PACKED ONE YOU WANT.

Okay, first of all, not all of you go for action movies, and not all of your women go for chick flicks. But a lot of times men and women prefer different movies, so that's what we're saying with this idea: go to something radically different from what you would normally watch just because your woman loves it. For the purposes of this description, consider it a chick flick.

You probably won't be the only man there. Thanks to women "dragging" their boyfriends and husbands along, men are actually a big audience for chick flicks. And sometimes you will be pleasantly surprised at the entertainment value of a chick flick—just don't go talking about it with the guys tomorrow.

ORGANIZE HER SHOES.

You know they are a mess in the closet. The fact that you've noticed that her shoes are unorganized and took the time to arrange them will earn you a lot of favors. Trust us.

> *A Story from Matt*
>
> *Okay, maybe this tactic is more for the OCD guys like me. I share a closet with my wife, so I felt much better when I did it, and she thought it was all for her. The next week, the shoes were everywhere again. Oh, well. I still got the points for doin' it.*
>
> *When you make an effort to make her environment the way she wants to see it, it demonstrates that you are thinking about the world through her eyes. All women want different things but loving her by seeing the world through her eyes is something EVERY woman loves.*

Make the bed for once.

A made bed is a turn-on for women. It shows you put in effort and that you care, and it's a nice little treat for her that night. She may not make the bed every day, either, so coming home to a made one is special. Don't get the pillows too right, though, or she is gonna want you to do it every day.

> *A Story from Spencer*
>
> *Keeping the house organized is something that is much more important to my girl than it is to me. There are many times that I have to be reminded to keep the house straight. Although I try, I still fall short of the way she likes the house to be. Instead of apologizing constantly and promising that you'll do better, take the time to go above and beyond. When you do this it build a little leniency for when you drop the ball.*

CLEAN THE BATHROOM.

This is only a one-time thing. You don't want to set a precedent that you're cleaning the bathroom every week for the rest of your life. You want to do it once really, really well, so she can't say that you've never cleaned the bathroom. Take selfies of you with rubber gloves on and all the cleaning supplies, and she'll never forget. Send her texts with the play by play as you are cleaning, with funny faces to keep her smiling all day.

Do the floors, mirrors and all. You may not think it's romantic, but she definitely will. This is a humility play. Being humble in this endeavor is super cute, and she will love, not like, that you did it. Plus, the bathroom will be clean now.

If you have money, you can get a maid, but you should then just say you had the house cleaned 'cause she is so dirty. Nothing wrong with calling a girl out on her messes. She will be doing that to you down the road, but you should do it yourself at least once, so you prove to her that you can get your hands dirty.

Change the Screensaver on Her Computer to a Pic of You as a Couple.

Choose a picture that will remind her of an amazing memory you two had. You can even stage a photo session. Can't decide among the shots? Well, then use the one of her having fun or smiling at the camera and you looking at her like the nut in love that you are. If you have already given her a physical photo, then write something funny on her screensaver.

CELEBRATE HER BIRTHDAY WEEK.

Starting six days before her birthday, give her a gift a day. She will love the buildup. For guys, this requires some major planning, so if you do this one, know you are in the ninety-ninth percentile of badass boyfriends. But it's totally doable. Here's how you break it down.

The day before day one, you want to make the arrangements for all seven days. You don't want to be scrambling last minute.

Day 1 (seven days before the birthday): Give her a card. Not one of those cheap-looking dollar ones either. One that's made of thick paper. If you don't feel up to writing a heartfelt message, make sure to choose a card that has a meaningful preprinted sentiment.

Day 2: Give her flowers. Earn bonus points by sending a bouquet to her work.

Day 3: Give her jewelry.

Day 4: Take her out for drinks. An end-of-the-day happy hour will make up for the fact that she has to work like a grown-ass adult on her birthday.

Day 5: Make dinner reservations.

Day 6: Present her with a cookie, cake, or cupcake with a candle in it.

Day 7: Give her *the* birthday gift.

To enhance all this, make love all seven days.

PERFORM THE SELFLESS ACT.

Do something nice for her and never let her know it was you.

Sure, we fix all the car problems and never tell our partners, but we're talking about doing something selfless that's not painful or sneaky, like going to the opera that you hate and not bitching about it but enjoying it, or at least pretending to enjoy it. Never let her know you didn't love the experience. That is true selflessness. If you can do something amazing and never tell her, then you should. You will know you did it for her and she will love that you did something together and that's what matters.

HAVE A RELATIONSHIP CHECK-IN CONVERSATION.

You don't want to be so arrogant as to think that you're always knocking it out of the park. Occasionally, you need to have an honest conversation with her and check in with how she feels you're doing in the relationship.

She may want more time with you or to be taken out more. She might want you to ask about her day, or she might want more sex. You don't know, bro—she may be a lot more sexually charged than you think. It's not enough to give her attention. You have to make sure you're giving her attention in the specific way that stimulates her.

Listen to her honest feedback and make the necessary adjustments. You want to make sure that you don't do this in the other phases of the relationship. If you haven't proven that you can anticipate her needs, then this conversation is going to sound weak and needy.

A Story from Spencer

My girl and I spend the begging and end of each day journaling together about how we want to show up in the world and for each other. This takes 15 minutes in the morning and 15 minutes at night. These 30 minutes make sure that nothing slips through the cracks. When you address how you're feeling on a regular basis, it makes it much easier to manage expectations before unsaid emotions build up and blow up and an unexpected time.

Another good exercise is for each of you to make 2 lists. List 1 is "What I'm willing to give", and list 2 is " what do I require". Make these lists separately and then go out to nice place to dinner and discuss the lists.

Compare what you are willing to give to what she requires in the relationship. If there is something that she requires that you didn't write down that you were wiling to give then you can have a conversation about compromise. This will help the expectation management of the relationship or it will reveal that you two aren't compatible. Better to know now before you get marriage and kids involved

Start telling her she is beautiful...every day.

A real man consciously recognizes how beautiful his woman is. She shouldn't be taken for granted for even a day. If you think you do take her for granted, then ask her if you do and see what her response is.

Be agreeable today.

Just go with it. Don't tell her you are going to be agreeable today, or you may end up roped into a whole different kind of day. Just be cool, and if you don't agree, don't argue today. She will notice. You can always unleash on the relationship tomorrow, ya dick.

Fix Your Tone

Record yourself in conversation with her. You can do so easily with the press of a button on your cell phone. Play it back for yourself later. Can you hear the dickishness in your tone and words? Yeah, cut that out. Go into your own self and fix yourself. Self-awareness is going to help you grow as a person and a partner.

Send an email with something sweetly written on it, like "thinking of us."

That's it. Just an email. To her personal email address. Playing gaga via her work address could get her in hot water, and nobody should be messing with another person's livelihood. If you do want to make sure she sees it while she's at work, keep it short, sweet, and tame. For example, you could send a cute hand-drawn picture of something you two have done. Basically, keep your masterpiece rated G if you send to her work address. You've got to be careful that you join her in her space, not invade her space.

DANCE PUBLICLY.

And by publicly, I don't mean you have to dance in front of other people. Do you know how much you'll make your girlfriend laugh (in a good way) if you grab her hand and jam with her down the frozen foods aisle of the grocery store, the motion sensors lighting up the freezer cases as you go?

Pulling her close in an elevator is perfect. And if you stop on a floor before yours, don't stop dancing even as others get on. Just hold her a little closer. A lobby—of a hotel, apartment building, or other such space—is also great. There will likely be other people around, but they won't be paying attention to you; the atmosphere is nice; and there's plenty of room for a twirl and a dip.

Do not pass up the opportunity to dance with her when your song comes on. In order to dance to your song, you need to have one—and you need to remember that you have one. This means that you need to pay attention—and maybe control the situation a little by making a song happen.

Remember to think about all the "firsts" that happened before they happened in the beginning: first dinner, first coffee, first kiss, first drive. Remember when that first happens, what's a song that's playing in the background? If you've been paying attention, then it should be in your notes. So remember it; maybe even comment about it later to her. It does no good if you privately thought one song was playing when you first kissed and she didn't notice or she remembers a different song.

Also, there's nothing wrong with giving your future self a little help. Is she coming over to your place for a drink, and you suspect the first kiss will happen? Put a select few songs on repeat in the background; that'll narrow down the options when you go to remember.

> *A Story from Matt*
>
> *I was walking with a girlfriend to the car after dinner one night, and the song that was playing when we had our first kiss came on the audio system piped outside the restaurant. I stopped right there in the street to slow dance with her. It was a simple way to step up the romance in the relationship. She talked about that moment with all her girlfriends for months.*
>
> *This is where your notes come in handy. When you remember the little things in the relationship, it holds a lot of meaning.*

Take an Impromptu Vacation.

Make use of a three-day weekend to get outta Dodge or even stay at home but act as though you're away—no errands. This is a great way to reconnect on the fly. Play in-city tourist or take a whirlwind trip outside the country (you can find some great last-minute deals). Here are some specific ideas:

- Pack her bag and have her driven to the airport blindfolded. From there, take her to Europe on a surprise vacation. The trip doesn't necessarily have to be somewhere far or exotic, but this kind of gesture adds spontaneity and excitement to the relationship.

- Let her know you want to take a trip and have her pick the destination. Tell her the budget, and she can do the work and surprise you with where you two are going. She just has to let you know what the weather is, so you can pack accordingly.

- Even if you want to keep the weekend plans a secret from your woman, make sure she knows you're planning something, so she keeps her schedule open. And then follow through. You do not get to bail on her because of work or something—she's adjusted her plans and gotten excited. She deserves follow-through.
- Stay a day late. She will be pleasantly surprised when she thinks the vacation is coming to an end, only to find out that you're starting your trip a day early or are coming home a day later. Make sure you've cleared all this with your bosses.

SET UP A BATH WITH SALTS, CANDLES, AND SOME CHOCOLATE OR WINE.

When your woman has had a long day, this can be a great treat. Once you've led her to this at-home spa, let her enjoy it alone. If she wants you to stay you can listen to her day's events while she soaks.

Keep in mind that you may set all this up, and she may not want to get in the bath. She may not even want to go see the surprise. That's okay. Don't get upset because you put so much effort and got no reward. Remember, you're doing this to make her feel good, so, ultimately, follow her lead. Look for another way to cheer her up or show your support, which may involve asking her what you can do or simply doing nothing. What she may need most is some space.

WAKE UP AN HOUR EARLY AND HAVE BREAKFAST TOGETHER.

There is something nice about waking up next to your partner. Maybe instead of rushing into the shower and out the door, slowly wake up together and start the workday with eggs sunny-side-up and a kiss. That first meeting will be far better.

It's okay if the best breakfast to be had is at your place, and that may even be better than going out. Wow her with what a nice meal you make with only a couple of eggs and some cheese. It's a lot about the presentation, so take a second to make sure the plate looks great. Tell your girl to stay in bed for twenty extra minutes while you get the coffee started. It's a simple gesture—throw in some granola and fruit, and you have just made her day. Check out some Instagram photos of homemade breakfasts for some ideas on plating the food. Make an effort and keep surprising her with new talents you have.

Have a fashion show.

When she comes back from shopping, you know she is going to want to show you what she got. Now you probably don't care, and most men don't, but women want to share their day with everybody, and you just happen to be in the house when yours came home, so turn lemons into lemonade and ask for a fashion show.

Sit in the living room or on the bed while she changes in another room. Make sure she tries on each outfit, one at a time. Encourage her to walk the hallway like it's a catwalk, turning at the end by you and making it sexy, even if she just bought new T-shirts. Throw some catcalls out there and enjoy the show. You should pick your favorite new piece of clothing and tell her to wear it to dinner Friday. Show her that you appreciate her, and you can take charge of a situation.

This is also another example of giving her something to look forward to and wearing something you were involved with. She will feel hotter knowing you picked the outfit and more confident knowing you already like it. Now, she is still going to ask you how she looks on Friday night. Just smile and try to have the same amount of excitement you did when she was modeling the outfit for you.

TAKE HER TO DINNER.

Set everything up yourself. For once, don't lean on her to make plans. You know enough to know a place that she will love. Think about the kinds of environments she lights up in and the attire she typically wears and take her somewhere accordingly. If she's all dresses and sparkles, you don't have to break the bank—take her to a family-owned Italian place, or even start the evening at a swanky hotel bar and then move on to something more affordable for the main meal. If she's a jeans girl, it's still not McDonald's—we're thinking a cool gastro pub. She will love that she gets to dress up in her comfort clothes. Don't drink too much. You will need to perform when you two get home.

PULL OUT HER CHAIR AT A PLACE OTHER THAN A FANCY RESTAURANT.

Keep it simple, keep it classy, and always treat her like a lady, no matter where you are.

> *A Story from Matt*
>
> *I happen to love Taco Bell, and a girl I was dating took me there for my birthday once. She even brought a table cover, which was pretty cute. I made sure we sat at the table with room for wheelchairs and mobility, which also gave us more room (don't worry—we would have moved if someone in need showed up). I pulled her chair out for her. It feels good to do it and just keeps the night moving in a positive direction.*

Most guys will act like gentlemen when they're in an upscale setting. When you bring upscale chivalry to an ordinary setting it becomes more meaningful

GIVE HER A BIG KISS WHEN YOU GET HOME.

Okay, so you've just finished a Monday. Meetings, phone calls, angry customers, demanding bosses, looming deadlines, definitely not the kind of sleep you had just a couple of days ago on the weekend, maybe even some arguing kids, and nothing in the house for dinner. All of that…and you and your lady exchange just a peck on the cheek? That's the definition of insanity. You two love each other; you're crazy about each other. To you, she's the hottest girl around. You are each other's rock.

This is what you do instead: give her a real kiss. Walk in the door, set down anything you're carrying (you want both your hands free for this), make her the only thing in the room that you can see, and give her a kiss. We're talking a slow, relax-the-lips, put-some-attention-into-it kiss. You can go as far as making out with her, right there by the front door. Let your hands go where you both want them to go. Who knows, it may lead to something more than kissing, and that is a great way to finish a work day.

What if she's been home a while, and when you get there, she's ass deep in laundry? That is not where either of you want her ass. You can't kiss her while she's folding socks. Her mind is on that. So, first, say something: "I'm going to help you finish this—later." And then throw her onto the laundry, still hot from the dryer, and kiss her. She may give stiff lips, so you will have to tell her to loosen them up. "Pucker up, buttercup" kind of lighthearted language may get the kiss you are going for.

But what if she's had a truly rough day at work or for any reason doesn't want to fall into bed with you right then? Listen to her. If you kiss her, and she steps back, go with that. It takes two to tango, and if you both hear what the other needs right then—read the body language—you'll be dancing later.

Go back to where it all started.

Take her back to where you had your first date or gave your proclamation of love and repeat the night. This is like home turf for you. It's a familiar zone where you already did it right once. Use the home-field advantage to rekindle those first-moment feelings and show her you remember where it all started.

SPICE UP AN EVENT.

We've all sneaked texts to our sweeties during boring meetings or made use of that plus-one just to have someone on our side at a tortuous company meet-and-greet. But don't forget to have some sexy times when you're feeling good too.

You can make it simple by assigning double meaning to a phrase you might normally say at that event, or up the ante by giving a special meaning to a word that will seem completely out of context to everyone else. Mentioning the quarterlies to your boss in front of your wife will make her smile because she knows that when you say "quarterlies," you're really asking her to go fool around in the car. If you're feeling more daring, go with the absurd. Hearing you respond to your co-worker's question about the last board meeting with something like "Well, the cinnamon scones they served were good" will drive your woman wild. Your co-worker will be left scratching his head at your goofy response, but your woman will know you cannot wait to get her home.

You don't have to actually follow through on your code words—just saying them stimulates the connection between the two of you. It really stimulates the situation if you do follow through, though! (One more tip: don't get caught.)

A Story from Matt

There was an annual event coming up that was known for good food and good music, but my wife and I wanted to spice it up a bit more. The day of the event I started texting her about how much I wanted her and that I may not make it through the event. She ate it up. I said things about taking her in the back room, public enough for a thrill, but just private enough to enjoy the thrill.

We came up with a code word that we would say or text if we found a room that would fit the bill. Throughout the night, we both had a little twinkle of anticipation in our eyes; having a coded sexual conversation in front of people made the night that much sweeter. It was also cute to watch her across the room and see her opening closet doors just to see what was inside.

It makes you feel more connected when you are living in your own little world in public. It's like your own little language that you two can understand. The more you build the concept of "us" the deeper the connection and the hotter the fire.

Develop some of those pictures of the two of you on your smartphone.

Women go nuts for pictures, so why not print one...or ten? Even if you don't have a printer with photo paper, getting those pics off your phone is as easy as emailing them to a store with a photo counter and picking them up the next time you're out. While you're there, earn extra points by buying a frame for one or two of them.

Give up guys' night.

Leave halfway through guys' night and come home to your girl early. Text her on your way, letting her know you're coming home to be with her instead of your friends. Don't make it sound like you weren't having fun, but simply that you miss her. This message says you chose her over your friends—which takes the threat of them away and ultimately allows for more guys' nights out!

Don't make a habit out of this one, as your boys may start to feel your girl is a threat. In fact, tell them the plan, and they will be much more forgiving.

CLOSING: SEE YOU OUT THERE

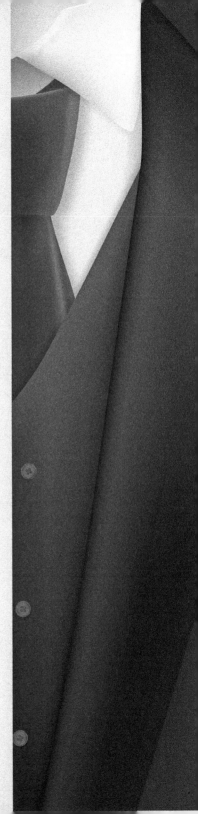

Before you dive in and start following this guide to be with you dream woman you first have to find the right woman. As guys, we tend to choose a woman based on her looks and how fun she is inside and outside the bedroom, but there is more to the relationship than that.

There are many women that you can see yourself being with but people change as the years pass. So you don't just want to find a woman that is good for you right now but you want to find a woman that can grow with you. This is why we suggest being with her for at least a full year or two before you really commit.

The honeymoon phase usually last for the first two years. For the first six months of a relationship everyone is on their best behavior. After the first year, you have seen each other through all the seasons and holidays of the year. You've gotten to see each other in your natural habitat. Between year one and two, not only have you seen the best and worst of each other but life will have thrown you enough curveballs to see how well you work together as a team to get through the chaos of life.

Even if you know the very first moment you meet her, don't

lose your balls by simply giving her everything that you want. Your relationship with your girl is a never-ending game.

Out in the dating world, you kept yourself busy by creating multiple experiences for multiple women. To have a successful relationship, you don't have to shut that instinct off. You just have to direct all of that energy toward one woman. The key is to not lose your identity and character but to adjust the settings of your attributes to stoke the fire of one woman instead of every woman.

The tips in this guide are meant to give you a head start on building your relationship, but they are also supposed to inspire you to come up with your own activities.

Finally, here's one more tactic:

CLOSING: SEE YOU OUT THERE

GIVE HER THIS BOOK.

Encourage your girlfriend or wife to fold down the corners on the tips she likes. Realize that she will now know your moves, though.

Now that we think about it, probably better to give it to your guy friends and keep the cool guys guide to yourself.

Once you have completed all five of these phases, the game doesn't end. In fact, it's just beginning. As your relationship continues, you have to make sure that it progresses. There is no "finish line" for relationships. They are forever going to change. You're going to change, she's going to change, and you both are going to change as a couple—and just because you stick together doesn't mean you're progressing. You have to always be living in some version of these five phases over and over and over again.

You wanted to be completely fulfilled. That's why you dated multiple women: one who was fun, one you could trust, one who was great in bed, and so on. To be completely fulfilled with one woman, you have to create all those dynamics in one relationship.

The secret to a long-lasting relationship is to continually pursue each other even though you have full certainty that neither of you is going anywhere. You are a hunter, and if you stop hunting your girl, your instinct will catch up with you and you will find yourself "setting the spark" with another woman. Once you set the spark with that other person, you're naturally going to try to get her hooked, and suddenly you will find yourself taking that relationship to the level which you're missing in the relationship you already have. It's a slippery slope.

Our natural urge to hunt strikes us when we feel alone, but in a healthy relationship, we're never alone. If you don't put intentional effort into seducing your woman, you are bound to stray. That's why you should refresh yourself on this book every six months, follow these tips that we've provided for you. Plus continue to be creative and add to your own list of moves.

You can't take the player out of the man. It's just the way we are designed to function. To deny wanting lots of great sex and wanting to be admired by women and play clever games to hook them is to deny yourself. Don't believe that you have to change who you are in order to build an amazing relationship with one great woman. You don't have to change who you are. You just have to change how you measure your success with women. If this woman is special enough that you've read to the end of this book, then start to change the way you brag to your friends. Be known as the player who is winning the game.

TROUBLESHOOTING

Of course you can't talk about games in the twenty-first century without using video games as examples. So in this final section, let's talk about when you need to troubleshoot your game. First, always remember your overall goals with each stage in your relationship. If you forget everything else, those alone will guide you on a smart path:

Set the Spark

Stand out from the pack.

Be a classic gentleman.

Keep her on her toes.

Allude to your softer side.

Get Her Hooked

Keep her off your top-priority list.

Become a part of her daily thoughts.

Solidify your sex life.

Hint at a future together.

Lock Her Down

Make her part of your plans for the future.

Integrate with her friends and family.

Develop unique roles as a couple.

Invest in the long-term.

Control the Flame

Be irreplaceable.

Set expectations for her and yourself.

Answer with brutal honesty.

Create space in the relationship.

CLOSING: SEE YOU OUT THERE

Fuel the Fire

Be romantically over the top.

Let your guard down.

Be agreeable.

Treat her like a queen.

OK, now, level up by remembering some tips to address common issues. We've structured this next part like an index. After each entry, which is an issue you may run into, we offer a little general advice and then direct you to some of the specific tips you may want to follow in this case. This isn't a comprehensive list, and one size very much does not fit all—you may find other tips that work even better in these cases for you and your girl!

Attention, needs some. Your woman is acting a bit like a kid on too much sugar. She's a little antsy for you to put all your focus on her.

OK, to fix this, you need to give a little but also piss her off a little. She's not really about to walk out on you; she just is kind of pouty and wishing she really were your princess. Give her attention, but in increments. Give her attention, but maybe in a more serious way than she anticipated—make this focus really count. And give her attention in a way that slows down her frenetic feeling, like doing something slow and meaningful, like building a time capsule. Here are just a few of the tips that may address her need for attention:

THE COOL GUY'S GUIDE

In Set the Spark: Initiate the five-minute video call; Ask questions that no other guy has asked her; Send her creative social media messages

In Get Her Hooked: Give randomly; Learn to piss her off and make her nervous the right way

In Lock Her Down: Create a time capsule

In Fuel the Fire: Organize her shoes; Have a relationship check-in conversation

Distant. She's acting distant. She needs a certain kind of attention to remind her how great you are.

This doesn't mean you slobber all over her or bend over backward trying to win her back. In fact, one of the tips we suggest for this issue is to disappear. But always remember, you're still doing things like being in the relationship even when she's not around.

In Set the Spark: Fix her hair; Surprise her with sweetness; Massage her head; Provide service after the sale; Walk with her as if it is a dance; Throw her robe and towel in the dryer before she takes a shower

In Get Her Hooked: *Really* tell her what you do for a living; Buy her some bubble bath and leave the container on the counter for her to find; Disappear when you aren't physically together; Be in the relationship when she is not around

In Lock Her Down: Cuddle naked; Don't dump her but allow her to leave

Headache, always has. Her interest in sexy time has evaporated.

Help nudge that interest back, in small but firm and interesting ways.

In Set the Spark: Write "I want your body" with your finger on the bathroom mirror before she takes a hot shower

In Get Her Hooked: Make love, have sex, *and* bang the hell out of her; Have sex at a drive-in; Keep a sexual idea board; Embrace in the elevator; Red light means stop—and make out.

In Fuel the Fire: Take an impromptu vacation

In charge, thinks she is. She's forgotten that you're both boss in this relationship.

Remind her in ways that both put you in charge of the situation and delight her, so she's rewarded for following your lead.

In Set the Spark: Order her dinner and drinks

In Get Her Hooked: Change the screensaver on her computer to a pic of you as a couple; Smack her ass during sex just a little bit harder this time

In Lock Her Down: For her birthday, go out to dinner, but have her friends meet at the restaurant for champagne after dinner

In Control the Flame: Ask her what her favorite part of your body is; Pick out her outfit; Give her an honest *and* constructive answer when she asks how she looks in that dress

Lack of variety, complaining about. She's tired of what she thinks is same-old dates and behaviors.

Change it up, in big and little ways, so she knows you're interested in keeping the spark alive.

In Set the Spark: Make reservations for late in the night, so you can be the last ones to leave

In Lock Her Down: Play tourist

In Fuel the Flame: Pull out her chair at a place other than a fancy restaurant

CLOSING: SEE YOU OUT THERE

Needy, acting too. She's focusing all on herself, and she doesn't like that you aren't as well.

Assure her she's important but remind her she's not the only important one in the relationship.

In Set the Spark: Initiate the five-minute video call; Plan the one-hour date

In Lock Her Down: Meditate together; No TV tonight

In Control the Flame: Don't let her tantrum turn into a fight; Support girls' night out

Tab, she keeps picking it up. The one who holds the purse strings holds all the power, and right now her wallet is determining everything you two do together.

Show how you're in control too, and when you do let her pay, make her buy something you specify.

In Set the Spark: Walk on the traffic side; Walk through a revolving door first. When it's windy, walk in front

In Get Her Hooked: Make a bet for Sunday brunch. Loser buys

In Lock Her Down: Make her a little care package

In Control the Flame: Ask her to make your favorite meal;

THE COOL GUY'S GUIDE

Do the dishes afterward; Give her a gift card to Victoria's Secret and tell her your favorite color; Have her buy you some socks

CPSIA information can be obtained
at www.ICGtesting.com
Printed in the USA
LVHW090917050719
623118LV00001BA/172/P